HV 713 Caregiving: A multidisciplinary
.C37 Approach
1981

DATE DUE

APR 0 9 1995

APR 1 0 1997

Mu

B

AUDREY COHEN COLLEGE LIBRARY
345 HUDSON STREET
NEW YORK, NY 10014

PALO ALTO, CALIFORNIA

AUDREY COHEN COLLEGE LIBRARY
345 HUDSON STREET
NEW YORK, NY 10014

PUBLISHED BY

R AND E RESEARCH ASSOCIATES, INC.
936 Industrial Avenue
Palo Alto, California 94303

LIBRARY OF CONGRESS CARD CATALOG NUMBER

81-51215

I.S.B.N.

0-88247-594-0

Copyright 1981
By
Carmela Hernandez-Logan

TABLE OF CONTENTS

INTRODUCTION.. 1

I. THE CAREGIVER.. 2
   The Key to Effective Caregiving: The Caregiver
      by Theo Pilot.. 3
   The Role of the Trained Caregiver in Quality Care
      for the Young Child by Deanna R. Tate................... 9
   The Nurse as a Caregiver in the Mainstreaming of
      Children and Adults with Handicaps by Peggy Drapo... 12

II. ESTABLISHED PRACTICES IN CAREGIVING...................... 21
   Interagency Coordination by Joene Grissom................ 22
   A Multiagency Cooperative Health Program: Can It
      Work? by Lois P. Case................................... 26
   A Private Practice in Parenting by Marion W. Pratt...... 37

III. PROPOSED PRACTICES IN CAREGIVING......................... 44
   Infant Stimulation Programs for the Handicapped:
      Rationale by Mary Jane Gitter........................... 45
   Recreation and Leisure Programming in Caregiving for
      the Handicapped by Claudine Sherrill.................. 50
   Providing Effective Care for the Aged by Cora A.
      Martin... 57

IV. SPECIFIC CONCERNS IN CAREGIVING........................... 60
   Promoting Pro-social Behavior in Children by
      Frank T. Vitro.. 61
   The Cultural-Linguistic Difference of Bilingual
      Children by Ysau N. Flores, Jr.......................... 65
   Randy: An Allergic Child with Reading Problems by
      Doylene R. Hogg... 67
   Nutritional and Feeding Problems of the Physically
      Handicapped by Janine DiVincenti....................... 71
   Nutrition and the Handicapped: Normal and Abnormal
      Processes of Eating by Jean Judy....................... 74
   Parent Counseling: Professional View and Parental
      Reaction by Donna L. Sumlin and Jamy Black-McCole... 79

AUDREY COHEN COLLEGE LIBRARY

BIOGRAPHIC NOTE ABOUT THE EDITOR

    Carmela Hernandez-Logan received her B.S. and M.Ed. degrees from Pan American University at Edinburg, Texas in the field of Elementary Education. Her Doctor of Philosophy degree is from The University of Texas at Austin in the areas of Early Childhood Studies/Child Development. Presently Dr. Hernandez-Logan is on the faculty at Texas Woman's University, Department of Curriculum and Instruction. Her teaching fields include early childhood studies, and educational evaluation/research methodology.

INTRODUCTION

Caregiving is everyone's concern. Each of us is involved in giving and receiving care during different phases of our lives. The involvement in caregiving may be as obvious as when a parent cares for a child, or as subtle as the caregiving that takes place between "equals" in our society. It must be emphasized that the chronology of caregiving has no specific beginnings or endings; only transitions. The differences that exist are based only in degree, relative to the level of self care for which any individual is responsible. Since caregiving involves all of us all of the time, it necessarily involves the skills and body of knowledge from many academic disciplines.

The first persons with which we come in contact in our life are usually doctors and nurses in a hospital setting. We then depend on our parents (or parent surrogates) to meet all of our physical, psychological, and social needs for several years. As we grow we begin to develop relationships which meet an increasing amount of our social needs. We also begin providing for the social needs of others. Educational requirements (those determined by law as well as by personal ambition) have also begun to be met by professionals charged with this responsibility. Although most of us become able to meet all of our physical needs, we remain dependent on our family, friends, and perhaps, school or job to meet some of our social and psychological needs.

Any time during this sequence of events an individual may minister to the needs of another human being in a variety of ways. Caregiving thus becomes an activity that permeates every aspect of society. In some cases, caregiving behavior may be overlooked because of its subtlety or because it has become such an integral part of human behavior (i.e., an infant's smile in response to a parent's caress; a child assisting another child; or an individual taking his/her turn at completing a household chore).

Human beings are multidimensional in personal and physical characteristics. Therefore, the agencies and institutions charged with the responsibility of caregiving must also be multi-dimensional.

The papers presented in this volume cover only limited areas of the entire spectrum of caregiving activities. The topics have been categorized beneath the following headings:
1. The Caregiver
2. Established Practices in Caregiving
3. Proposed Practices in Caregiving
4. Specific Concerns in Caregiving

Categorization was undertaken for the convenience of the reader and also to provide a framework by which those charged with the responsibility of caregiving could begin to view it as a multidimensional phenomenon.

I

THE CAREGIVER

The papers in this section present information on the qualities, competencies, and roles of "trained" caregivers in a variety of settings. The term "trained" caregiver is used in a special way. It is not the purpose of the authors to give the impression that only an individual who has received special training can qualify as a bona fide giver of care to his/her fellow beings. The intention, rather, is to convey the idea that an individual's basic competencies in caregiving can be improved through training, given that the motivation to improve is there.

THE KEY TO EFFECTIVE CAREGIVING: THE CAREGIVER

by Theo Pilot

The philosophy and practice of effective caregiving, as the focus of the conference, makes some specific hypotheses necessary. The hypothesis I will offer is "to provide effective care, the capable caregiver should be educated in the same mode and manner that are shown in effective caregiving."

This statement requires some defining. First, the area of effective caregiving will be limited to the care of young children in group care - day care, nursery school, kindergarten, etc. Effective caregiving will be defined as the care which meets the individual child's developmental needs - social, emotional, intellectual, and physical. Third, the capable caregiver is a person who has the skills and individual capabilities to provide effective care for young children in groups.

The Caregiver

The capable adult who cares for the young child shows characteristics that have been defined in several ways. Mille Almy (1), in The Early Childhood Educator at Work, lists warmth, nurturance, patience, energy, likes to work with adults, abstract attitude, and maturity, as important qualities for adults who work with children. The teacher is a model who demonstrates expected behavior, facilitates exploration and investigation of materials, and comforts in distress, Almy states.

Klein (6) in "Toward Competency in Child Care" discusses the Child Development Associate (CDA) competencies that are in six broad areas of knowledge and skill. The CDA competency areas are: (1) Safe and healthy learning environment; (2) Physical and intellectual competence; (3) Positive self-concept; (4) Positive functioning of children and adults in a learning environment; (5) Coordinate home and center child-rearing practices and expectations; and (6) Supplementary responsibilities.

These items give some insight into professional thinking concerning adults who work with children. To summarize, the effective caregiver is a model who has a positive self-concept and the knowledge and abilities to make choices and decisions to help children grow and develop.

Adult Education

The education and training for those who work with and teach young children has been traditionally the college or university campus. Since the surge of day care, beginning with World War II, there has been need for more and more care for younger and younger children in group settings. Head Start, the Department of Health,

Education, and Welfare, and the community colleges have helped bring training and education to those who require and request it as they are working with young children.

Traditional classes, as most of us remember from our earliest years of school, and through college, have been for the most part, lecture, with some discussion and an occasional media presentation. The teacher imparts information, the student memorizes it, writes it down, gives it back to the instructor. It is then <u>learned</u>; I doubt it. Bruner (2) in <u>The Process of Education</u> says that the first object of any act of learning, over and beyond the pleasure it may give, is that it should serve us in the future. He further states that learning should not only take us somewhere but also allow us to go further more easily.

Jones (5) discusses the Piagetian theory that beginning stages of any learning must take place through direct sensory experience with concrete objects for the experiential base of later conceptual understanding. Although adults are capable of formal operations, Piaget's terminology for advanced stages of learning, Jones thinks that age should not be a considered factor, rather developmental sequence of learning, regardless of age, should be the consideration of learning as each person has to personally reconstruct knowledge.

Instructors should provide a model for the learning process of the student. It is difficult to provide a model for learning, the one you wish students to use as they work with children. The adult trainer/instructor must value the individual and possess the attitude of being a caring person to impart this to the student.

The competent teacher-educator, like the effective caregiver, has to know the individual to provide appropriate learning experiences. Like young children, the adults have varying knowledge levels, experiences and capabilities as it is important to teach neither up or down to the adult students. This premise, that we must meet individual adult differences in learning styles, makes the modelling adult teacher role primary to all teacher training plans.

A parallel will be developed showing areas for the planning of a developmental program for young children and the same areas used for planning for the education of adults. In other words, as the adult learns, so learns the child. The parallel that is proposed includes five areas that will be discussed in the following.

<u>Information and Appraisal: Planning Education and Care</u>

<u>The child</u>. For children, the particular philosophy of the program gives built-in requirements. Within a framework of the individual school or center program the teacher/caregiver begins <u>with</u> the child <u>for</u> the child. Some evaluative process is basic to planning for the child. Evaluation in terms of age level development of infants, preschoolers, and older children often is used as the basis for planning programs. Other personal observations give the teacher/caregiver information for planning to meet growth and

development needs of the child.

The adult. The adult teacher/educator always begins with certain requirements of the school, college, university, or training requests that give evaluative guidance. College courses have structured requirements that may be age, class attendance, objectives, degree plans, etc. Requests for training such as Head Start staff training may specify "outdoor play for three, four, and five-year-olds," and this makes implicit that evaluation has been made by the person requesting training. The teacher-educator, like the child caregiver, makes further evaluation to plan for the student. From this information, detailed planning is made for both group and individual training activities.

Environment: Room Planned for Care and Learning

The child. The setting for young children in school and day care varies depending on the program philosophy, age of children, and other factors. The environment is the key to the child's learning. The young child learns by being involved with the materials that are available; therefore, it is important that the environment be planned and structured to provide opportunities for active participation. The environment provides security as the child knows where things are and how they can be used; provides a social setting for interacting with friends and adults; meets physical needs of health and safety; and includes activities and materials that promote growth and development.

The adult. An accepting attitude that makes the student comfortable is important. The teacher-educator provides an environment that is conducive to learning as the instructor is aware of the individual needs. As a variety of instructional techniques are used, the teacher-educator plans different structuring of the environment. Comfortable chairs, eye-level seating, areas and plans for movement when "hands-on" learning is taking place are all considerations for the instructor who is providing the modelling training of adults.

Routines and Schedules: Time and Tempo for Learning

The child. For the child in a group setting, routines provide security. Flexible scheduling is part of the caregivers most important task in providing effective caregiving for young children. Flexibility within a set routine is essential for the child's well-being as well as for group functioning. The routines that include meals, toileting, nap, and rest, as well as active and quiet times with appropriate activities, are part of daily life in any program for young children. The caregiver's role in providing routines is to plan the times to meet the needs of the children - physical requirements of food and rest; active and quiet periods that are times for the child; and schedules that include time for creative exploration, time outside each day, imaginative play, science and music.

The adult. The competent instructor provides for the adult in training a similar flexible schedule to meet needs. The class or workshop schedule is planned to provide time frames and activities that allow for individual learning styles. Time plans for adults can show a semester calender so each student has the course requirements in hand. Students can then have time to prepare work at their own pace. Knowledge of time expectations for completion of work to be turned in and work to be done in class or group activities, gives the adult security as well as establishes trust between the instructor and student.

Objectives and Goals: The Why and What for Teaching

The child. Setting objectives depends again upon the program, the child, the family, and society. Goals may be as varied as social group play in a half-day nursery to complete comprehensive child care that includes dental care and psychological evaluations. Goals for the child are part of every program that provides effective child caregiving. Objectives for individual children within a program are essential for planning and providing the proper setting and activities to meet the developmental needs of the child and the program objectives. Goals for young children in effective caregiving are based on the following developmental needs: (1) emotional: for security, affection, acceptance, consistency, self-concept building; (2) intellectual: for information, independence, responsibilities, creativity; (3) physical: for good nutrition, motor activities, sleep, rest, and a balance of active and quiet times; and (4) social activities; for choices, encouragement, respect of rights and companionship. Goals and objectives provide the base for evaluating the quality of caregiving and education.

The adult. The teacher-educator gives clearly defined objectives for courses and other training. Goals for education can be clearly stated in information given to the student. Objectives and requirements set by the college for courses can be supplemented by the student's personal goals and expectations. Objectives for workshops and other training activities should be clearly defined. Goals and objectives for adults are seldom defined as meeting individual needs. By allowing students, in course work, to specify objectives in addition to stated college guidelines, provides for a method of individualization of goals. Activity-oriented workshops should specify objectives for the participants so they and the trainer have common knowledge of expectations of the training.

Activities: How To

The child. A well-planned environment is one set by the caregiver to provide the child a panorama of activity choices. Some activities will be individual - looking at a book, working a puzzle; some activities will be small group - building with blocks, listening to a story; some things will be large group - music, a field trip. The effective caregiver provides activities that give the child some thing to do as the group moves from one activity time to another during the routines of the daily schedule. Transition activities are a necessary part of a good program for young children. The ultimate plan for activities is to provide the materials, the interactions, the time, and the space for child exploration in a secure environment that allows for individual choices.

<u>The adult</u>. The student who is taking a course can also be given a scenario of activity choices. The teacher-educator who is providing education in ways that develop skills and knowledge in "hands-on" activities, makes available many and varied opportunities. Readings, audio-visual presentations, relevant peer discussion, teacher-student discussions, games, field trips, lectures with concrete examples, active art and music, and role playing are the kinds of activities that provide a model for the active participation in which young children learn. Adults who learn through this method, one that has modelling as a primary mode, are better able to teach in this way when they provide care for young children.

Evaluation: What Was Accomplished

<u>The child</u>. We have come full circle from the beginning appraisal used to plan for the child. Evaluation of learning is an ongoing activity for the child caregiver. Children are learning constantly; therefore, evaluation is done day by day as there are successes and accomplishments. Children are learning as they participate in activities in verbal interactions with adults and peers and as they use materials available. Periodic observation of the child, to assure needs are being met, is necessary to evaluate effective caregiving. Evaluation provides the evidence of goal achievement for each child and for the program.

<u>The adult</u>. Adult evaluations are varied. Ongoing evaluations, made by the teacher-educator as the student participates in activities are important. Completion of assignments and post-assessments measure growth and knowledge. Effective modelling education evaluates to assess learning. Self-assessments help measure the effectiveness of training provided by the teacher-educator.

Summary

The premise is that those who are receiving training and education for becoming professionals in the early childhood education field will provide more effective care and education for children if they receive their training and education in the same mode and manner that effective care shows. The teacher-educator provides the model for this learning. Provide adults with experiential learning and they are much more likely to provide this kind of learning environment and experience for the children they care for and teach.

    What we hear, we forget.
    What we see, we remember.
    What we do, we learn.
This is an old Chinese proverb that is basic to my beliefs about

learning and knowing. Let students _do_ as we adult educators provide the model for the effective care we want for all children.

NOTE: Theo Pilot is associated with the Texas Department of Human Resources, Early Child Development Division, Dallas, Texas.

REFERENCES

1. Almy, Millie. _The Early Childhood Educator at Work_. McGraw-Hill Co., 1975.

2. Bruner, Jerome S. _The Process of Education_. Vintage Books, 1963.

3. Gilbert, Dorothea. "Educational and Growth Needs of Children in Day Care," _Child Welfare_, Vol. XLIX, January, 1970.

4. Honig, Alice. "Training Caregivers to Provide Loving, Learning Experiences for Babies," _Dimensions SACUS_, January, 1978.

5. Jones, Elizabeth. "Teacher Education: Entertainment or Interaction?" _Young Children_, Vol. 33, March, 1978, No. 3.

6. Klein, Jenny W. "Toward Competency in Child Care," _Educational Leadership_, October, 1973.

7. Moustakas, Clark. _Teaching as Learning_. Ballantine Books, Inc., 1972.

8. Spodek, Bernard. "Early Childhood Education and Teacher Education: A Search for Consistency," _Young Children_, Vol. XXX, No. 3, March, 1975.

9. _The Primer_. Child Day Care Association, Inc., 1972.

THE ROLE OF THE TRAINED CAREGIVER IN QUALITY CARE
FOR THE YOUNG CHILD

by Deanna R. Tate

When one considers the dimensions of quality care for the young child, one immediately thinks of terms as the facility, the learning environment, motherly teachers, TLC, or some such. What is the most important determinant of quality care? I believe, alone with many other professionals, that it is the competency of the child's caregiver. I also believe that competency in caregiving can be influenced through training. Now hear me correctly, persons can be competent caregivers without formal training; however, even these have received training through modeling, i.e. behaving like, other competent caregivers within their life experiences. The other side of the coin is that for those who are motivated to learn from it, training can be the means for improving competence in caregiving.

The types of training programs for improving competence fall into two types: (1) preservice-training which occurs before the person begins functioning in the role of caregiver, and (2) inservice-training which occurs after the person begins functioning as a caregiver of young children. Preservice training usually is that which we mentally associate with more formal settings such as schools. Examples are high school programs which teach parent education or occupational care to high school age youth, and college level teacher training programs which presume that the student has had no, or limited experience in a caregiving role. While not minimizing the usefulness of these organized training programs, I maintain that inservice training is far more potentially powerful. I have been an educator in both types of programs, and my observation has been that the experience of having caregiving responsibility serves as a motivator which aids the learning process.

Inservice training, to be effective, must be relevant, give immediate feedback, be planned jointly and regularly scheduled, and give enough quickly achieved improvement of successful practices with young children to maintain interest in learning. Content for instruction in caregiving is much more easily secured - books and audio-visual materials abound - than is information about implementing the inservice educational process. One resource that is helpful in this regard is Polly Greenberg's book, <u>Day Care Do-It-Yourself Staff Growth Program</u> (The Growth Program, 1975).

Inservice training is provided by employers, by regulatory agencies, by professional organizations, and by educational institutions. The qualities one looks for in a provider of training are the competency of trainers, the regularity of the training, the stability of the instruction or organization as a provider of training, and the ability and willingness to be responsive to the needs of caregivers. The training opportunities in a community can be discovered by contacting departments of human resources or public welfare, local community colleges with child development programs, or members of local affiliate groups of organizations such as the Association for the Education of Young Children. Most programs are provided from moderate to no cost to participants.

One final area of concern is the recognition of the competent caregiver of young children. Historically, child care has been a lowly-paid occupation, and it remains so to this day. The result is a highly mobile workforce, since child care is a very demanding occupation, and teachers tend to "burn out". Basically the demands of the occupation and the rewards secured are out of balance.

The next challenge of the early childhood development profession is to take steps to develop a system whereby competence in caregiving can be properly rewarded both monetarily and non-monetarily. I'm please to say that some progress is occurring in this area. The Child Development Associate Credential is a recognition of competence as a caregiver of three-to-five-year-old children. Credentials are also awarded for bilingual-bicultural caregivers of three-to-five-year-olds. In the planning stages are credentials for caregivers in home settings, called family day home caregivers.

In Texas, professional organizational representatives are working on a plan to integrate and organize existing recognitions of competence and to fill in the gaps for other caregivers not covered under credentialling systems as CDA. Our dream is to make it possible for employers to know explicitly the competencies of caregivers they employ, and thus, to reward the most capable in the organization's own merit and personnel advancement system. In this way, the monetary situation for competent caregivers should improve without placing undue burdens on employers. The workforce would be stabilized, and children would be experiencing better caregiving at the hands of more competent caregivers.

In the meantime, I must encourage all of you to recognize competent caregiving in as many ways as your creativity can devise: a pat on the back, congradulations for a job well done, a half-day off on one's birthday, a "caregiver of the week" board (identifying the meritorious behavior which warranted the naming), asking the competent caregiver to share a skill in a staff meeting, and so on. There can never be too much of this type of recognition. We all like to know that we are valued members of our reference groups. One caution. Be sure you are recognizing <u>competence</u>, not just providing social rewards indiscriminately; otherwise, these encouragements lose their potential for fostering competence in caregivers of young children.

In summary, let me make the following points. Competence in caregiving is an essential ingredient in quality care for young children. Training is a means for increasing competence. Inservice training is a powerful means of training which is provided at a low cost by a variety of organizations in local communities. Steps are being taken to recognize competence in formal ways, in hopes that this will lead to increased monetary rewards, but in the meantime, we need to use as many non-monetary forms of recognition as possible to encourage the competence of caregivers. In this way, the quality of care for young children can be improved with society as a whole as the beneficiary.

NOTE: Deanna Tate is on the faculty in the Department of Child Development and Family Living at the Texas Woman's University at Denton.

THE NURSE AS A CARE GIVER IN THE MAINSTREAMING OF CHILDREN AND ADULTS WITH HANDICAPS

by Peggy Drapo

One of the most controversial problems in education today is the mainstreaming of physically and/or mentally handicapped students. The issue is not in whether to do it - for Public Law 94-142 demands it - but the issue is, how it shall be done. As schools begin to implement the law, the literature is beginning to reflect problems and successes which surround mainstreaming.

In essence, Public Law 94-142 states that:
1. Handicapped persons must be provided a free appropriate public education.
2. Handicapped students must be educated with non-handicapped students to the extent appropriate.
3. Education agencies must identify and locate all unserved handicapped children.
4. Evaluation procedures must be adapted to ensure appropriate classification and educational services.
5. Procedural safeguards must be established.

Failure to comply with these regulations means that the school will be cut off from all federal assistance to state and local agencies.

Naturally the classroom teachers, whose experience has been that of dealing with the so called "normal" child and problems encountered by these children, (which are great enough to keep the most dedicated teacher hopping) are overcome by the implications of this law to their classroom. Suddenly they must look at a new population of children, who, until now, have required specialized teachers and specialized classrooms. Who are these children and what does the law mean by handicapped?

The handicapped, as defined by the act, are children and adults who are:
1. mentally retarded
2. hard of hearing
3. deaf
4. orthopedically impaired
5. other health impaired (example: pregnancy, deaf blind, multi handicapped)
6. speech impaired
7. visually handicapped
8. specific learning disabilities

Most educators are appalled at the notion of the hours of special attention even one of these children would mean in a classroom that is already extremely busy. The issue of accountability, which is a popular topic in the literature impressing teachers of their legal responsibility, is a hundred fold more frightening at this point. What is education of the handicapped and what does this mean to the educator who is in the field - away from sources of teacher education and instruction? What does it mean to the colleges and universities educating future teachers? Can we look at the education of an individual who also happens to have a disability and see first the human and secondly the handicap? We must. Where does it all start?

A Starting Point: A Meshing of Professional Abilities

Administration can begin the successful transition of children with handicaps coming into the public school program by helping the various members of the mainstreaming team understand the law. It is to them the team looks for inservice program planning, clarification of the law and time schedules to begin implementation in a manner that will be in the best interest of the child.

Membership of the team include:
1. Therapist (O.T., P.T., speech and recreation)
2. Classroom teachers
3. Family
4. Nurse
5. Administrators
6. Speech consultant
7. Guidance counselor
8. Psychiatrist and psychologist
9. Physician and orthodontist
10. School social worker

Each member brings a specialized body of knowledge and one team member cannot function as well without the other. The law, however, brings with it certain implications for all of us. It will change a great deal of the school team's daily routine and, for some, mean extensive inservice.

For those of us preparing professionals as providers of health care, it means we must be mindful of what mainstreaming will be to those who must cope with it - the child, the teacher and the family. For some professionals it will only mean a change in the setting of their work. For others it will mean a change in the way they prepare practitioners. The teacher and the school administrator cannot achieve the true concept of mainstreaming without a great deal of input from many health care providers, and it is our responsibility to help meet these needs by preparing professionals who are capable of functioning in this area.

The Preparation of Nurses

Many schools and colleges of nursing preparing future nurses deal with physical and mental disabilities which we see in mainstreaming, but they do it within the context of hospitals. Children come to the hospital for braces, casts, surgery, medical regulations and diagnosis. More often than not, they are ill when they arrive or shortly after admission will be recouperating from some procedure. The nurse who sees the child only in this way is hampered in seeing the true impact of the disability on the family. Their time is limited with this patient on a medical floor.

The teacher, the therapist, and the family see the child in a different environment - a state of wellness which includes the disability. In essence P.L. 94-142 states that criteria for selecting handicapped pupils for mainstreaming are in terms of filling educational needs of the child and the capability of the program to meet the child's needs rather than focusing upon the physical, mental, emotional or other handicap. When one has seen the person who is handicapped only in context with that handicap or accompanying illness, it is not easy to use that experience to help the child meet normal needs. Of course, hospital nursing experience and care of the child with handicaps in that setting is invaluable, but the needs of the child that the nurse can meet far exceed that situation.

Here at the Denton campus we do not use the hospital totally for the instruction of nursing students in the care of children and adults with neurological and/or mental disabilities, endocrine and psychosomatic disorders. One semester of the senior year is spent at Denton State School for the Mentally Retarded and the State School's Community Adjustment Program. We have also begun to place students in the Early Childhood Education Program of the Denton Independent School District. That program is located here on campus working with pre-school children with disabilities. These experiences give the nursing student a complete picture of the total care needed by the child from infancy to old age - plus the needs of the family. We are learning a role the nurse can fill as well as roles other professionals use when interacting with the child and family. When the semester is complete, the student has learned to do:
1. Health assessments which include a problem list as well as assessing the client for skills (or lack of them).
2. A plan of care to assist the client in meeting his/her needs.
3. Implementing that plan.
4. Evaluation of nursing care.
5. Revision of the plan.

The student also is involved throughout this process with health teaching and research of the literature to document care and search for new ideas to apply to nursing. Basically, the part that I am most enthused about is that while the student is learning about the signs, symptoms, syndromes, problems, needs, or other related textbook pictures, they are learning something equally important. They are learning to communicate, and they are becoming increasingly aware of the importance of health maintenance and the value for clients to be as independent as possible. Before the student leaves the course, most of them have worked through many ethical and value judgements.

Nursing as a Resource to the Classroom Teacher

Emotional Disorders. The Texas Education Agency Policies and Administrative Procedures defines emotional disorders as including these problem areas:
1. Learning disorders which have no basis in intellectual, sensory or other health related factors.
2. Unsatisfactory interpersonal relationships because of inability on the part of the child to develop or continue those relationships with peers and significant others.
3. Feelings and behaviors which are inappropriate even in normal situations.
4. A depressed or unhappy condition which is general in nature.
5. Psychosomatic complaints, pain or fear which have a basis in the school situation or in personal problems. (23, 23-25)

Background in psychiatric nursing, OB, pediatrics, and medical-surgical nursing prepare nurses to work with the mainstreaming team in effectively overcoming many of the child's problems. Very often these children are on medications whose side effects can be interpreted to the teacher. Often children who are not on medication or in treatment should be, and the nurse can assist the teacher in bringing these problems to the parents' attention.

A thorough background in growth and development assists the nurse in observing for problems related to certain maturational problems. Juanita Fleming looks at the maturational levels in which certain emotional disorders arise. Beginning with infancy and early childhood, she states that failure to thrive, infantile autism, and childhood schizophrenia are encountered. Pre-school and early childhood, on the other hand, are problematical in psychotic behaviors, psychoneurosis, hyperkenetic activity, withdrawn or anxious characteristics, unsocialized aggression and finally runaway behavior. In late childhood and early adolescence she sees the all too familiar pattern of drug abuse or suicidal activity. (12, 146-160)

Learning Disabilities. Learning disabilities are described as a block to learning in one or more of the processes we attribute to the ability to learn. Problems can occur in the auditory or visual mechanisms. The nurse who is skilled in the screening for hearing and visual disorders will assist the teacher in diagnosing the underlying causes of the child's learning problems. She can alert the teacher to specific behaviors which a child with hearing impairment will exhibit.

Mental Retardation. Mental retardation exists not only in functioning more than two standard deviations below the mean or average of intelligence tests, but also in problems of adaptive behavior as measured on behavioral scales. Only those who are impaired in both areas are considered retarded (23, 20-22). Nurses who have experience working with the mentally retarded very often find that children and adults can minimize their problems if behaviors can be improved. Work on appropriate behavior starts in early childhood or infancy as it does with any child. Institutionalization, no matter how good that institution is, can lead to many maladaptive behaviors which mainstreaming would hope to prevent. An adequate nursing program gives nursing students opportunity to work with clients in social adjustment, body image, nutrition education, dental hygiene, grooming, sex education and personal safety and accident prevention. A nurse with this background is cognizant of techniques to teach retarded individuals skills and behaviors that will make them more acceptable to themselves as well as others.

<u>Physical Disability</u>. Physical disabilities can cover a long list of disorders, some of which also include mental retardation. A few of them are:
    Cerebral palsy
    Spina bifida
    Diabetes
    Tuberculosis
    Allergies
    Muscular dystrophy
    Post-encephalitic neurologically impaired
    Epilepsy
Nursing education has thoroughly covered these disorders and nurses are a ready resource to the teachers. The concern for reading, writing and arithmetic will now be coupled with what will happen to Johnny's skin if he sits too long in a wheelchair without repositioning and how will we plan a bladder and bowel program for him? Handling and positioning as well as feeding techniques are important factors to consider with young students who have cerebral palsy. The teacher will appreciate input from nursing in relation to correct feeding techniques, and bowel and bladder programs. Medical data are not essential pieces of information that the teacher needs to know from medical clinics from which the child comes. The nurse can assist the teacher in soliciting instead, information which delineates communication skills, emotional behavior, intellectual functioning, specific motor and sensory functions, and information about neurological problems such as epilepsy which will have bearing on his classroom experience. (8, 394)

<u>Who Will Be An Advocate</u>?
The literature declares that the retarded and disabled need advocates. Who is an advocate and what do they do? In some charitable models or in some helping agencies, help comes on a "take it or leave it basis", in which the handicapped have no voice or are presented as "poor souls" or "innocents", and "angels" who are kept in a dependent situation. These are not what we mean as advocates.

Contrary to the models above, an advocate has been described as one who recognizes those dependent making processes. Independence is to be desired and an advocate helps the person choose those things which will help free them of the need for charity. Human service is a right - not a charity. An advocate understands experiences and feelings and tries always to treat the person with a handicap as an equal who wants to live and work within the normal population. Anger, not pity, is the expression of the advocate who finds those with handicaps being dealt with in a manner which takes away from their selfworth. Creating change becomes the vocation of the advocate.

Being an advocate is not without cost. They must plan on being criticized by those they question, but, of course, an advocate will return activism for opposition. How can one go about being such an advocate? By writing, forums, meaningful activity recognized as a symbol, boycotts, education, negotiations, lobbying, being involved in model programs, legal assistance to the client, and finally, helping to take the mystery out of handicapping conditions. (3, 309)

The Nurse as an Advocate for the Handicapped and the Teacher

Though the thrust of mainstreaming is to turn from categorizing students with labels, physical, mental, and maturational needs must be met in order to help the child become successful. Handicapped students bring to the classroom many individual health needs above and beyond those of "normal" children which have direct bearing on success in mainstreaming.

Early intervention poses a problem in that in the crush of trying to provide intervention for the child, the crisis needs of the family are sometimes not met. The nurse is ideally suited to deal with this aspect of care since that has always been a thrust of nursing. The nurse is educated to fucus on the infant's developmental needs and abilities and is able to bring the two together which will assist the teacher (20).

The disability often cannot be removed and while the child is being normalized, he will never be "normal". The nurse can work with parents, understanding their needs in relationship to their feelings about what this disability means to the family unit. Help in coping with this aspect will assist them in letting him progress at his own rate and enhance his potential (13).

The school nurses' role should be broad enough to encompass certain activities and skills related to mainstreaming. Some of them are emergency situations, education of staff to handle children with acute problems, continuous preventive health care for the children, teaching normal growth and development as well as those serious chronic problems, a plan of complete care for all children who have health needs, and finally, collaborative planning with other professionals and agencies to manage the child with disabilities. (9, 34)

Some of the conditions the nurse is prepared to deal with are those of cerebral palsy, seizure disorders, visual disorders, hearing impairments, structural malformations, chronic respiratory diseases, genetically acquired conditions and mental retardation with a multiplicity of causes. Her psychiatric background also covers those students with psychiatric disorders or emotional problems.

Nurses who are educated to work with the disabled have the ability to counsel the young person about their health problems and to treat or prevent other disabilities from costing that person independence. For the spinal cord injured client, the matter of skin care is, for instance, of utmost importance and its neglect can cost the student months of lost school time (10).

Teachers need help with children's need for special diets, medications and treatments throughout the course of a normal day. Mainstreamed children with PKU disease, diabetes, and cystic fibrosis are examples of this. Children who have shunts for hydrocephalous will need monitoring as well as children who have spina bifida and are on a program of intermittent catherization. The nurse can assist the child to maintain a successful school program in spite of these physical needs.

An unrealistic proportion of school coverage and heavy pupil work load for the school nurse is detrimental to her being actively involved in developing good school health programs. Each school where mainstreaming occurs should have a full time nurse with at least a baccalaureate education and preferrably a master's preparation. Her role should be re-examined with the implications that mainstreaming will now bring. A school nurse with adequate clinical and theoretical background will highly effect the outcome of the mainstreaming program in a positive way.

School administration should explore the role of the nurse in more depth. She is there to serve the child who is not handicapped also, and with proper background the nurse clinician or the practitioner is fully capable of both (5). Higher education programs need to examine their preparation of nurses educated to administer health related programs in the school. Research needs to be done in the role expectations of school administrators and teacher educators for that of the school nurse. As mainstreaming moves forward, so will the need for the nurse as a member of the educational team.

NOTE: Peggy Drapo is on the faculty with the School of Nursing at Texas Woman's University at Denton.

REFERENCES

1. Ballard, Joseph and J.J. Zettel, "Law Review: The Managerial Aspects of Public Law 94-142". *Exceptional Children*, March 1978, 44, No. 5, 457-462.

2. Bigge, June L., <u>Teaching Individuals With Physical and Mental Disabilities</u>, (Columbus: Charles E. Merril Publishing Co.) 1976.

3. Biklen, Douglas, "Advocacy Comes of Age", <u>Exceptional Children</u>, March 1976, 2, No. 6, 308-313.

4. Blackwell, Marion Willard, <u>Care of the Mentally Retarded</u>, (Boston: Little, Brown and Co.) 1979.

5. Blust, LaDelle Crane, "School Nurse Practitioner in a High School", <u>American Journal of Nursing</u>, September 1978, 78, No. 9, 1532-1533.

6. Cantrell, Robert P. and Mary L. Cantrell, "Preventive Mainstreaming: Impact of a Supportive Service Program on Pupils", <u>Exceptional Children</u>, April 1976, 42, No. 7.

7. Cohen, Shirley and others, "Law Review: Public Law 94-142 and the Education of Preschool Handicapped Children", <u>Exceptional Children</u>, January 1979, 249-284.

8. Cruickshank, William M., <u>Cerebral Palsy A Developmental Disability</u>, (Syracuse: Syracuse Un. Press) 1976.

9. Del Campo, Ethel and Diane B. Josephson, "Accomodating the Severely Retarded Child in Our Schools", <u>American Journal of Maternal-Child Nursing</u>, January-February 1978, 34.

10. Drapo, Peggy J., "A Hostel for the Handicapped", <u>American Journal of Nursing</u>, September 1978, 78, No. 9, 1530-1531.

11. "Education of Handicapped Children Implementation of Part B of the Education of Handicapped Act", <u>Federal Register</u>, August 23, 1977, U.S. Office of Health, Education, and Welfare, Washington, D.C.

12. Fleming, Juanita, <u>Care and Management of Exceptional Children</u>, (New York: Appleton-Century-Crofts) 1973.

13. Harris, Merril, "Understanding the Autistic Child", American Journal of Nursing, October 1978, 78, No. 10, 1682-1685.

14. Harvey, Jasper, "Legislative Intent and Progress", <u>Exceptional Child</u>, January 1978, 234-237.

15. Holm, Carol S., "Deafness: Common Misunderstanding", <u>American Journal of Nursing,</u> November 1978, 78, No. 11, 1583-1585.

16. Lepler, Marcia, "Having a Handicapped Child", <u>American Journal of Maternal Child Nursing</u>, January-February 1978, 32.

17. Martin, Edwin, "Some Thoughts on Mainstreaming", <u>Exceptional Children</u>, November 1974, 150-153.

18. McMillian, Donald L. and Melvyn I. Semmel, "Evaluation of Mainstreaming Programs", <u>Exceptional Children</u>, September 1977, 9, No. 4, 1-14.

19. Reynolds, Maynard C. and Jack Birch, <u>Teaching Exceptional Children in all America's Schools,</u> (Reston, Va.: The Council for Exceptional Children) 1977.

20. Stevens, Harvey A. and Rick Heber, <u>Mental Retardation, A Review of Research</u>, (Chicago: University of Chicago Press) 1972.

21. Stroud, Marion B., "Do Students Sink or Swim in the Mainstream?", <u>Phi Delta Kappan</u>, December 1978, 316.

22. Syder, Lee and others, "Integrated Settings at the Early Childhood level: The Role of the Nonretarded Peers", <u>Exceptional Children</u>, February 1977, 43, No. 5, 262-266.

23. TEA Policies and Administrative Procedures.

24. Tudor, Mary, "Nursing Intervention with Developmentally Disabled Children", <u>American Journal of Maternal Child Nursing</u>, January-February 1978, 25.

25. "What the Laws and Regulations Require", <u>Today's Education</u>, November-December 1977, 54-56.

26. Wyatt, Diede Schmidt, "Phenylketonuria: The Problems Vary During the Different Developmental Stages", <u>American Journal of Maternal-Child Nursing</u>, September-October 1978, 296-302.

27. Ziegler, Suzanne and Donald Hambleton, "Integration of Young TMR Children into a Regular Elementary School", <u>Exceptional Children</u>, April 1976, 42, No. 7.

II

ESTABLISHED PRACTICES IN CAREGIVING

The focus of this section is based on the idea that one of the loftiest goals of caregiving is to encourage and establish the interdependence of individuals and services in the giving of care. Each author presents information on existing facilities that strive to attain the goal of interdependency and cooperation between education agencies, medical facilities, parent-training services, and individuals seeking assistance from them.

INTERAGENCY COORDINATION

by Joene Grissom

Agreements conceptualized in terms of service integration often break down when one begins to put it into operation. An underlying purpose of service integration is to develop a frame work within which ongoing programs can be coordinated and enriched to do a better job of making services available within the existing commitments and resources. Integration arises out of the growth and extensiveness of human services programs and the corresponding desire to deliver those services in an efficient and effective manner.

The Education of the Handicapped Act, Part B, as amended by Public Law 94-142, states that part of the responsibilities of state administration is to develop written agreements between state agencies concerning state educational agency standards and monitoring (121a.600). This reflects the desire of Congress for a central point of responsibility and accountability in the education of handicapped children within each state. This provision is included specifically to assure a single line of responsibility with regards to the education of handicapped children and to assure the responsibility must remain in a central agency overseeing the education of handicapped children, so that failure to deliver services is squarely the responsibility of one agency.

Service integration can be examined from four perception levels: (1) service delivery level, (2) agency/programmatic level, (3) policy level, and (4) organizational level.

Service delivery focuses on the services rendered to clients whose objective it is to provide a comprehensive array of services to meet the clients' total needs. The programmatic level shifts from the relationship between the provider and client to the relationship between autonomous agencies and programs. At the level of policy development, the focus is the role of general purpose government to pull together the strands of various programs within the increasingly complex intergovernmental system to achieve coherence and responsiveness in human services. The organizational structure focuses on the reorganization or creation of government structures designed to facilitate the other dimensions.

Each of the four dimensions of services promotes system improvement and development in its own particular way. The ideal model would be to include all four dimensions in order to achieve full service integration.

It is extremely important to keep in mind, that if service integration is to occur, the question of _why_ and _what_ be pondered from the very beginning. This may prove to be one of the most single important factors behind success.

Elements that need to be addressed in interagency agreements are:
1. Description of basis for developing the written agreement.
2. Definitions for agency or program-specific terms used in the agreement.
3. Description of purpose to be achieved through agreement.
4. Mutually agreed upon goals and/or onjectives of the agreement.
5. Eligibility criteria/description for population to be serviced or affected by the agreement.
6. Delineation of specific roles and responsibilities of each party to the agreement.
7. Mutual/shared responsibilities of all parties to the agreement.
8. Specific actions to be taken relative to the program/service identified in agreement.
9. Specific services to be provided by each party.
10. Designation of responsible party or liason person for implementation of agreement and functions of that role.
11. Specification of meetings (time, dates, frequency).
12. Specification of reporting mechanism between parties of the agreement.
13. Confidentiality assurances relative to sharing of information.
14. Agreement among parties for notification in cases of changes.
15. Specification of time period for agreement to remain effective.
16. Schedule for periodic review of agreement.
17. Procedure for modifying or terminating written agreement.
18. Additional assurances.
19. Specification of additional incentives to be provided as a result of the written agreement, i.e., funding additional staff, work space, etc.
20. Signatures of all parties involved in agreement.

There are three classes of interagency agreements in which to incorporate these elements. They are as follows:

Class 1: Agreements about program standards. The first and most important class of agreements centers on common or baseline standards for conduct of programs which are similar, but are offered by different agencies. Such agreements are promises by these agencies to adopt common criteria for providing specific services to handicapped children and their families. Essentially, common criteria reflect multiple agency adoption of understanding about "who does what to whom, when, how, under what supervision, and to whose advantage." Promises which address such standards are prerequisite to any and all other agreements regarding the provision of services to persons with handicaps and their families.

Class 2: Agreements about allocation of resources. The second class of agreements consists of promises regarding the allocation of various agency resources in the accomplishment of mutually agreed upon objectives. There are at least six methods of cooperatively allocating resources.

1. <u>First dollar agreements</u>: When a handicapped person or his/her family is eligible for certain services from two or more agencies, a promise is made regarding which agency pays first.

2. <u>Complementary dollar agreements</u>: When a handicapped person or his/her family is eligible for certain services from two or more agencies, a promise is made for each agency to pay for certain services.

3. <u>Complementary personnel/dollar/agreements</u>: When a handicapped person or his/her family is eligible for certain services from two or more agencies, one agency commits personnel to serve the person directly while another agency reserves sufficient funds to pay for other services.

4. <u>Shared personnel agreements</u>: When children are screened prior to entering public schools, apromise is made which allows public health nurses and school nurses to work together in administering some health portions of the screening program.

5. <u>Shared facility agreements</u>: When children screened prior to entering public school, a promise is made to use a community hospital facility for carrying out all or part of the program.

6. <u>Shared equipment and materials agreements</u>: When children are screened prior to entering public school, apromise is made to use hospital equipment and/or materials for certain elements of the screening program.

<u>Class 3: Process and activity agreements</u>. The third class of agreements includes promises of uniform processes, forms, and activities by multiple agencies offering comparable services. Agreements regarding standards (Class 1) and allocation of resources (Class 2) are absolute pre-requisites to process and activity (Class 3) agreements. Promises can be made regarding areas of activities which might be managed cooperatively. Each of these areas directly links the needs of individual persons and their families to the capacity of the cooperating agencies to respond. These services agreements can be addressed in a systematic manner if the promises clearly articulate how each carry out their responsibilities.

It is evident that service integration warrants a multidimensional strategy. To adopt and implement service agreements in terms of process and product, the need for conceptual model building in order to account for the variables that arise is strongly stressed.

Commitment on the part of the service providers is a crucial element in the coordination of services. Setting and reaching service standards will be the primary goal of service integration in providing comprehensive services.

NOTE: Joene Grissom is a consultant in Early Childhood Education with the Texas Education Agency, Austin, Texas.

REFERENCES

1. R. Audette Associates, 25 Chamberline Road, Chelmsfords, Massachussettes, 01824.

2. Dimensions of Services Integration: Service Delivery, Program Linkages, Policy Management, Organizational Structure. Human Services, No. 13. Dekalb: Northern Illinois University, Center for Governmental Studies, Project Share, 1979.

A MULTIAGENCY COOPERATIVE HEALTH PROGRAM:
CAN IT WORK?

by Lois Case

It has long been recognized in this urban community that a gap has existed in the provision of services to infants seen as being at high risk for developmental disabilities or for abuse and neglect. Pediatricians at the county hospital have been particularly concerned about those infants treated in the neonatal intensive care unit who are lost to follow-up after discharge from the hospital. Less than 60% of these low-income families keep their appointments at the hospital outpatient pediatric clinics. Since many of these babies are not seen at the public health department well-baby clinics, either, cases of developmental delay go untreated and are not recognized until the children are approaching school age. By then, the best opportunities for remediation have passed. Related to this is the higher risk of abuse and neglect associated with the interruption of the bonding process after birth (Kennell, Voos and Klaus, 1976), and with the difficulties in raising the child with physical problems (Kennell et. al., 1976).

The Process

Accordingly, in the spring of 1978, representatives of several concerned agencies met to discuss the problem. It was determined, after a series of meetings, that several components would be essential in providing an effective high-risk infant program:
1. A system for monitoring the progress of high-risk infants.
2. An aggressive outreach service.
3. A strong parenting education program.
4. Early treatment for physical and developmental problems.
5. Provision for case and program evaluations.

Consensus was attained that the program should provide medical, psychological, social, and educational services for each child identified as being at high risk until each child was at least of school age - a weighty undertaking. Since it was immediately apparent that no single agency had the means to provide such a comprehensive program, a cooperative effort evolved. A child services agency agreed to assume the leadership role for the program by providing the director, a pediatrician, an outreach worker, and a system for keeping records. The city health department offered the facilities of the neighborhood centers for special well-baby clinics, as well as nursing services. The regional Mental Health/Mental Retardation Authority agreed to provide a child psychologist for developmental assessments, and the State Department of Human Resources provided funding through the Protective Services Division. All children treated in the neonatal intensive care unit of the county hospital would be automatically referred to the program. Other agencies subsequently joined the project, including a parenting guidance center, a family planning agency, an educational service center, a physical disabilities treatment center, and a school for teenage mothers. Each agency agreed to contribute services, in varying degrees, to the program. The decision to engage in longitudinal research in conjunction with the program prompted the involvement of a faculty member of a local university.

After the director was hired in mid-July, 1978, the informal weekly planning meetings continued. However, as new agencies joined the Child Development Program, and as the need for structure became essential, several committees evolved: the Program Committee, comprised of all agency representatives who would be having direct patient contact; the Research Committee which included all representatives interested in participating in research; and the Education Committee, comprised of outreach workers and parent educators interested in coordinating and developing new educational efforts. Meetings of the general membership have since been held monthly.

One of the major challenges facing the program during these early months was the formulation of a system of communication and record keeping that would be adaptable to multiagency usage. It is probably safe to say that such a system has yet to be perfected, but it has been greatly enhanced through the use of a computerized tracking program. This system provides a record of patient activities as related to each of the participating agencies, as well as current demographic data. In addition, a chart containing all written reports is maintained on each child.

The Program

The enrollment of the first babies launched the program in mid-November, 1978. Several times a week, an outreach worker from the child services agency reports to the neonatal unit of the county hospital where she receives referrals of new patients. She then contacts the mothers, whether they be at the hospital or at home, and introduces the program to them. Although participation in the program is voluntary, approximately 90% of all mothers agree to participate, and sign the necessary consent and release forms. After the child is discharged from the hospital, the outreach worker contacts the city health department so that a visiting nurse may make a home visit. At that time, the child is given an appointment to one of the Friday afternoon well-baby clinics conducted by the public health nurses. The pediatrician and the child development specialist are in attendance at that time for consultation and examination of infants who may not be progressing satisfactorily. In any event, all infants are scheduled to be seen by the pediatrician when they are 3-4 months old. The pediatrician then determines frequency of clinic visits. After each clinic a staffing is held to determine future treatment plans for each child seen that day. In attendance are the pediatrician, child development specialist, nurses, outreach workers, and parent trainers. All mothers receive parent training individually or in small groups each time they attend clinic. To encourage attendance, they are given small gifts for their babies or themselves, provided by various service organizations. Mothers who do not keep their appointments are contacted by an outreach worker, who makes every effort to resolve the barrier preventing treatment for the child. No infant is dropped from the program because of lack of motivation on the mother's part, until at least three home visits have been made and all resources exhausted.

In addition to the infants who are referred by the county hospital, the Child Development Program also accepts referrals from professionals in the community, of infants born at other hospitals who are at risk for developmental delay or for abuse and neglect. These referrals stem from concern arising from behavioral observation, environmental factors, and parental factors as documented in the child abuse literature (Helfer and Schmidt, 1976).

It is anticipated that 300 infants will join the Child Development Program each year. If each child is followed until the age of eight, as is expected, the membership will reach 2,400 before it begins to level off. Partial funding for the program has been obtained from the Developmental Disabilities Council, the United Way, and various small foundations. For the rest, the Child Development Program is dependent on the continued support and involvement of the participating agencies. Can it survive? What are the barriers, and the strengths, of such a program?

The Literature

The Need for Cooperative Health Programs.
It is generally acknowledged that health service delivery in the United States is fragmented, duplicated, impersonal, limited, and selective (Aram and Stratton, 1974; Mailick and Jordon, 1977; Reid, 1965). Reid (1965) contends that "unmediated" coordination, referring to voluntary cooperation between agencies, has become less frequent in recent years. Aram and Stratton (1974) aver that successful interagency coordination in the health service area is an infrequent event and that documentation of such effort is even rarer. Indeed, this writer's experience in reviewing the literature would confirm their observation. Shiffman and Morrissey (1968), in describing optimal medical care services, would advocate
1. An integrated team approach to the care of the individual.
2. A broad spectrum of services, extending from prevention through rehabilitation.
3. A coordinated community health system with continuity at each level of medical care between physician, hospital, and health agencies.
4. Integrated hospital-based services, so that ambulatory and acute facilities are parts of a continuum.
5. Continuing programs of evaluation in terms of both quality and relevance to community needs.

Further, these same authors (Shiffman and Morrissey, 1968) remind the reader of the serious manpower problems that affected all of the helping professions in the 1960's, and the need for creative program implementation. This acknowledgment is even more relevant today. At the conference on "Early Intervention with High Risk Infants and Young Children" sponsored by the President's Committee on Mental Retardation and the Association for Childhood Education, the Community Development Committee included in its recommendations that programs be developed to provide high quality services to greater numbers of high risk children and their families in rural and urban poor areas (Wiegerink, 1976).

Theoretical Framework. In a well-known conceptualization of exchange interorganizational relationships, Levine and White (1970) describe the elements necessary for a community health organization to achieve its goals: clients, resources in the form of equipment and specialized knowledge, and the services of people to direct these resources. Few agencies have enough access to all of these elements to enable them to meet their objectives fully. Therefore, they must establish relationships with other organizations, to some degree, to function effectively. Organizational exchange may thus be seen as an effort by two or more organizations to achieve their respective goals or objectives through mutual action (Levine and White, 1970). The interdependence of the agencies in the exchange system is contingent upon three factors: (a) the accessibility of each organization to necessary elements from sources outside of the health system, (b) the objectives and functions of the organization, and (c) the degree to which domain consensus exists among the various organizations (Shiffman and Morrissey, 1968). The degree to which an agency is dependent on other agencies is influenced by its identification as a corporate or as a federated organization. Corporate organizations, those which delegate authority downward from the national or state level, are less dependent than federated units which delegate authority upwards from the local level. Corporate organizations as a rule, have more resources available to them through their parent organizations than do federated organizations (Levine and White, 1970; Sills, 1957). There can be no exchange of elements among agencies unless there can be agreement or understanding concerning the goals and functions of each agency. Any agreement made between agencies must rest on prior consensus regarding domain. Obviously, two agencies claiming the same domain will have greater competition and more difficulty in reaching consensus than will two agencies with complementary domains. Of crucial importance to consensus in a multiagency system is the resolution of the problem of "who gets what for what purpose" (Gillespie and Perry, 1975; Levine and White, 1970; Reid, 1969). Achieving domain consensus may therefore involve negotiation, orientation, or legitimation. When an agency's functions are diffuse, readjustment and compromise may be achieved through negotiation. If the agency's functions are more specific, an orientation or explanation may be all that is necessary.

A final alternative in obtaining consensus would be an enforced one, such as legitimation through licensing (Levine and White, 1970).

Many researchers have commented on the conditions necessary for successful coordination. Gillespie and Perry (1975) suggest that there be a clear set of goals, an established center of power, adequate facilities, trained personnel, and a well-developed administrative structure. O'Sullivan's study (1977) supports the observation that cooperation takes place if organizations have complementary goals and their administrators have similar backgrounds. Davidson (1976) makes the observation that interdependence can occur as the result of an initial cooperative effort and can create its own momentum for continuation. Also, those projects which hold out the promise of improving a given agency's resources have the greater chance of success. Reid (1969) cites two major strategies that may be employed to increase interdependence: facilitation and induction. Facilitation, effective when the agencies are nearing interdependence, relies basically on the coordinator's leadership and communication skills to serve as a liaison, mediator, and negotiator. When agency independence or conflict is such that facilitation is rendered ineffective, inducement will be required if coordination is to be achieved. Inducement requires that major changes occur in the goals or use of resources through power or influence. The inference to be drawn is that the effectiveness of inducement is limited by the amount of outside influence available. Also, the effects of such an approach would be quite circumscribed and subject to collapse once the pressure is withdrawn.

Admitting that cooperative programs are complex and difficult to coordinate, Levine, White and Paul (1969) express their belief that the more an agency makes its resources available to other agencies, the more valuable it will become to them.

<u>A Model Program</u>. Of particular interest to this author was a paper by Aram and Stratton (1974) describing a successful twenty-agency planning project to provide services to the elderly. Although the Child Development Program has progressed beyond the planning phase, there are a number of interesting comparisons to be made.

The planning project for the elderly had its roots in an informal exchange of ideas among representatives of several agencies providing services to the elderly. Through this process came the recognition that there was a "convergence of interests," independent but compatible, in the problems of the elderly. The Child Development Program experienced a similar beginning, with representatives of the county hospital, the city health department, the regional Mental Health/Mental Retardation authority, the Protective Services agency, and the child services agency playing instrumental roles in determining the nature of the new program. Each of these agencies had a vital interest in high risk infants, although their goals differed. They perceived their roles, then, as complementary.

Another finding in the Aram and Stratton Study (1974) was that, although twenty agencies were involved, a relative few took leadership roles. Those individuals considered key figures by general consensus, were also known to have attended the greatest number of general and committee meetings, and to have had early involvement in the program.

A review of Child Development Program minutes, combining general and committee meetings, reveals that the following individuals were most involved as evidenced by meeting attendance (December 1978 - June 1979).

		Meetings Attended
1.	The program director (Child services agency)	31
2.	Parent trainer (Mental Health/Mental Retardation Authority)	30
3.	Social worker (Child services agency)	27
4.	Social worker (City health department)	25
5.	Secretary/outreach worker (Child services agency)	23

Tabulation by agency (December 1978 - June 1979):

		Person/ Meetings
1.	Child services agency	125
2.	Mental Health/Mental Retardation authority	67
3.	Parenting guidance center	45
4.	City health department	27
5.	University	22
6.	Family planning agency	19
7.	Department of Human Resources	18
8.	Education service center	3
9.	County hospital	3
10.	School for teen-age mothers	2
11.	Physical disabilities treatment center	2

The agency which had agreed to assume the leadership role, the child services agency, has had almost twice as much involvement as any other agency. Of the original five agencies, four have remained at least moderately involved in the on-going process of the program. These figures, however do not represent informal contacts, nor do they necessarily represent the greater issue of power and control.

Aram and Stratton emphasized the fact that efforts at cooperation must meet the needs or interests of relevant persons; cooperation is a means through which various people and agencies can move toward their separate goals. "Convergence of interests" is a dynamic process, affected by numerous unrelated changes occurring within the participating organizations. Individuals and organizations who are aware and alert to these changes might enhance their opportunities to benefit from the "convergence of interests" when it occurs (1974).

<u>The Child Development Program</u>

One of the early tasks of the director of the newly-formed

high-risk infant program was to seek out suitable models for the
multiagency cooperative program. Documentation of successful cooperative projects of any kind is a scarce commodity, much less one
so specific as a high-risk infant project. Shiffman and Morrissey
(1968, p. 86) suggest that, in place of models, human service agencies
develop their own "custom designs" for their programs, with creative
implementation, based on their accumulated experience, rather than
mass production. Recognizing that a wealth of experience, skills,
and resources were available to us, we have created our own "custom
design." We will see now how well it fits into accepted community
and health organization theory.

Agency interdependence, as suggested by exchange theory, is
contingent upon accessibility of resources, objectives and functions
of each agency, and domain consensus. The resources lacking, as
each agency considered a longitudinal high risk infant program,
were the costly outreach services and a monitoring system. The
functions and domains of each agency, for the most part, were clearly
defined:

- County hospital: Inpatient, emergency, and specialized clinic care.
- City health department: Well-baby care, immunizations, nutrition.
- Child services agency: Evaluations, counseling, genetic and infant stimulation programs.
- Parenting guidance center: Counseling, parent education.
- Mental Health/Mental Retardation Authority: Family Services, evaluations, counseling.
- Department of Human Resources: Protective services for children.
- Family planning agency: Family planning.
- Education service center: Educational coordination and resource finding.
- School for teen-age mothers: Education, counseling.
- Physical disabilities treatment center: Physical therapy, speech and audiological services, infant stimulation program.
- University: Research

Since there is domain overlap among those agencies offering counseling, parent services, and infant stimulation programs, frequent
role negotiations will be necessary as the program grows (Gillespie
and Perry, 1975; Levine and White, 1970; Reid, 1959). Although
Levine and White (1970) and Sills (1957) draw a distinction between
corporate, federated, and private agencies concerning the need for
interdependence, this program has not substantiated their claim.
Of the five agencies, which still maintain the most power, three
are corporate (Mental Health/Mental Retardation Authority, Department of Human Resources, health department), one is county (hospital),

and one is private (child services agency). Reid (1965) and O'Sullivan (1977) have described various mechanisms for control of coordinated programs. Since the Child Development Program is a voluntary, cooperative effort, decisions are made through interagency conferences and allocations of coordinating responsibilities. The issue of power and interstaff relations will be more fully discussed in the next section.

Findings

Four major areas of interest have surfaced since the inception of the Child Development Program: (a) power and control, (b) interagency staff roles, (c) communication and coordination, and (d) program philosophy. Each will now be addressed in more detail.

Power and Control. An allusion has already been made to the fact that those individuals who are most involved with the program are not necessarily those with the power to make policy decisions. In fact, it has been a typical procedure, in most cases, for the administrator or director of an agency to initiate contact with the Child Development Program and to negotiate that agency's role in the cooperative effort. From that point on, liaison with the program is shifted to a staff person, who frequently does not have the authority to make agency decisions. This process has resulted in the need for informal contacts between agency administrators and the program director. It is through these contacts that most policy decisions are made.

All agencies are not created equal. Those agencies in possession of unduplicated resources, such as the county hospital and the city health department, have considerably more control over policy decisions (even with the hospital's low process involvement) than do those agencies which share domains. While no one agency can be considered indispensable to the program, decisions to leave the program by certain agencies would create serious disruptions.

Interagency Staff Roles. Several researchers (Aiken and Hage, 1968; Mailick and Jordon, 1977; Reid, 1965) have commented on the role conflict experienced by agency staff members placed in coordinated programs. Indeed, one of the most common questions concerning the Child Development Program is, "What, exactly, am I supposed to do?" This is a valid question, yet one that is most difficult to answer. The answer begins, "It depends..." It depends on the goals of the program, the goals of the agency, the time available by that representative, the time available by other agency representatives, the number of clients needing service at that time, and the type of service needed. It depends on the whims of funding and other environmental events concerning all cooperating agencies. As an example, the Child Development Program has been provided with eleven parent trainer-outreach workers from four different agencies. They are available to the Child Development Program varying amounts of time (ranging from 12-40 hours per week), have differing agency objectives, and differing professional orientations. There have been a number of agency staff reassignments, and frequent "close-calls" in funding reductions. Coordinating their efforts has been a task, at least weekly, since the inception of the program.

It is important, also, that each agency, and particularly the coordinating agency, have a clear understanding of the functions and administrative structures of the other participating agencies. In a program which depends on cooperation for its existence, it can be particularly damaging to use the "wrong" contact person, or to give inaccurate information concerning a member agency.

Communication and Coordination. The reader must be aware by now of the vital role that communication plays in a multiagency program. The literature has acknowledged the disadvantages of cooperative programs in terms of the amount of time spent in coordination. This paper has included a tally of the number of meetings attended by representatives of each agency. These figures do not include the vast number of informal contacts which go uncounted. Close contacts must be maintained with agency representatives on all levels, not only to coordinate plans, but to keep interest and enthusiasm alive. From these informal contacts come some of the most valuable assets that a cooperative program can have: mutual understanding and friendships. As agency representatives work together, rivalry and "turfism" tend to diminish as true partnerships evolve.

Program Philosophy. Few researchers have commented on one of the major requirements of a complex program such as the Child Development Program: the need for flexibility. Since agencies are cooperating voluntarily, and since most of them are involved in numerous other programs, the program is always at risk for funding and staffing cuts. The director who insists on rigid rules and structure is doomed to a life of frustration. Director and staff alike must be ready to fill the void, or "make do" when such set-backs occur.

Since the coordinating agency, the child services agency, has minimal power in the form of resources or outside influence, the director has little "clout" to enforce her demands. Rather, she must depend on diplomacy and a willingness to consider seriously alternative methods of approach. Fortunately, most of the participating agencies have been given a mandate to provide services to high-risk infants and are motivated to more toward interdependence.

A Final Word

The literature concerning cooperative ventures is almost uniformly pessimistic (Davidson, 1976; O'Sullivan, 1977, Reid, 1965). It has been suggested that agencies will not involve themselves in cooperative programs unless they have no other alternative, that such programs are costly in terms of staff time, that conflicts can easily arise over domain rights, and that staff members can be torn by mixed-role demands, these admonitions have validity. The future of a program like the Child Development Program might be tenuous and uncertain. Yet, the Child Development Program appears to be succeeding.

Its goals are being met, in a cost-efficient system. The participating agencies are cooperating, without coercion and with enthusiasm. Plans for program expansion are underway. It may not be meant to be, but it is!

NOTE: Lois Case is associated with the Child Study Center in Ft. Worth, Texas.

REFERENCES

1. Aikin, M. and Hage, J. Organizational Interdependence and Interorganizational Structure. *American Sociological Review*, December, 1968, 33, 912-929.

2. Aram, J.D. and Stratton, W.E. The Development of Interagency Cooperation. *Social Service Review*, 1974, 48 (3), 412-421.

3. Davidson, S.M. Planning and Coordination of Social Services in Multiorganizational Contexts. *Social Service Review*, March, 1976, 117-135.

4. Gillespie, D.F. and Perry, R.W. Influence of an Organizational Environment on Interorganizational Relations. *American Journal of Economics and Sociology*, January, 1975, 34, 29-42.

5. Helfer, R.E. and Schmidt, R. The Community-Based Child Abuse and Neglect Program. In R.E. Helfer and C.H. Kempe (Eds.) *Child Abuse and Neglect: The Family and the Community*. Cambridge, Mass.: Ballinger, 1976.

6. Kennell, J., Voos, D., and Klaus, M. Parent-Infant Bonding. In R.E. Helfer and C.H. Kempe (Eds.) *Child Abuse and Neglect: The Family and the Community*. Cambridge, Mass.: Ballinger, 1976.

7. Levine, S. and White, P.E. Exchange as a Conceptual Framework for the Study of Interorganizational Relationships. In H.A. Schatz (ed.) *Social Work Administration*. Council on Social Work Education, 1970.

8. Levine, S., White, P.E. and Paul, B.D. Community Interorganizational Problems in Providing Medical Care and Social Services, In R.M. Kramer and H. Specht (eds.) *Readings in Community Organization Practice*. Englewood Cliffs, New Jersey: Prentice-Hall, 1969.

9. Mailick, M.D. and Jordon, Pearl. Collaborative Practice in Health Settings. *Social Work in Health Care*, 1977, 2 (4), 445-454.

10. O'Sullivan, Elizabethann. Interorganizational Cooperation: How Effective for Grassroots Organizations? *Group and Organization Studies*, 1977, 2 (3), 347-358.

11. Reid, W. Interagency Coordination in Delinquency Prevention and Control. In M. N. Zald (Ed.) *Social Welfare Institutions*. New York: John Wiley and Sons, 1965.

12. Reid, W.J. Inter-Organizational Coordination in Social Welfare: A Theoretical Approach to Analysis and Intervention. In R.M. Kramer and H. Specht (Eds.) *Readings in Community Organization Practice*. Englewood Cliffs, New Jersey.

13. Shiffman, B. and Morrissey, E.F. New Models for Community Action in Providing Health Services. In F. Haselkorn (Ed.) *Mothers-at-Risk*. Perspectives in Social Work 1 (1). Adelphi University School of Social Work, 1968.

14. Sills, D.L. *The Volunteers: Means and Ends in a National Organization*. Glencoe. Illinois: Free Press, 1957.

15. Weigerink, R. Report of the Community Development Committee. In T.D. Tjossem (Ed.) *Intervention Strategies for High Risk Infants and Young Children*. Baltimore: University Park Press, 1976.

A PRIVATE PRACTICE IN PARENTING

by Marion W. Pratt

In spite of living and job environment which fragment today's families and communities, a society which offers parents little status or support, and the current pursuit of freedom to "do one's own thing," many courageous and intelligent persons choose to have children. According to Michael Novak (1), this decision demonstrates their willingness to accept the responsibilities of growing-up. He also sees the family as a stronger factor in educational success than the formal education agencies in the country.

The family as religious instructor, Novak asserts, does more for spiritual imagination than the churches. He states that wise political and social planning begin with the axiom, "What strengthens the family, strengthens society."

Recognition of the importance of family life is usually followed by the realization that there is seldom any preparation for it. We study, plan, prepare for almost everything in life except the most intricate of all our relationships. Nothing we do will take more time, money, and energy than our parenting. Yet nothing we do will have been prepared for so haphazardly.

The concept of parenting (though the word may seem ungrammatical) is becoming more widely accepted because it seems to give voice to a new awareness of relationships. There are many definitions of parenting. The Group for the Advancement of Psychiatry maintains that parenting includes more than the idea of caring for, nurturing, and educating children. It also encompasses consideration of the thought processes of parents, their expectations and goals apart from their children, and the recognition that parenting is itself a stage in adult growth and development (2). According to this group, the experiences inherent in rearing children usually compel individuals toward more complete self-development as human beings. Development is a process that never stops; however, its quality, at any age, is dependent upon circumstances.

When serious problems develop, the significance of family experiences are widely acknowledged. Yet prevention of these difficulties appears to be primarily the concern of certain professionals who recognize that the ultimate mental health of an individual is related to the feelings, attitudes, value, and practices established in the home by the parents. These specialists also understand that preventing the factors which constrain growth may be accomplished more easily, with less time and expense, than treating problems once they develop.

The parent in the home seldom realizes how vital he or she is to the quality of the child's future life. Parents usually expect to rely upon doing what comes naturally. If problems arise, they try to work them out within the home - just as their parents did (4). Asking for help may be tantamount to admitting failure as a parent, and as an adult. This is especially true of the mother who, many people believe, was born with special skills and knowledge about child rearing. This myth has been perpetuated for generations and simplifies the question of where to assign blame for a problem child. Today's liberated mother realizes that parenting is learned by <u>both</u> sexes and she refuses to accept total individual responsibility for success or the lack of it.

Being a parent today is more difficult than it was in the past. Today there are more pressures, more choices, greater financial costs, less direct control over families, a lack of consensus on values of how to raise children, and a declining respect for the vocation of parenthood. Family and community support are often minimal or on-existent. More and more parents, distrusting their own experience or lack of it, are turning to the churches, schools, medical experts, and the media for guidance. There are many "how to" books, written from various points of view, which try to simplify a very complex subject. As a result, parents often become more confused, guilty, and anxious. Six week and semester courses given on and off campus attempt to inform parents about the growth and development of an ever changing organism, their child. There are never enough answers, and answers that were true at one point in the child's life may no longer suffice even a few months later.

Thirty years of dealing with and teaching about infants and children have convinced me of the extreme complexity of human organisms. Just when you have them figured out, you realize that they have changed. Parent education, therefore, is not only necessary, <u>it must begin before the child is born and continue throughout the parent's life</u>. Ira J. Gordon envisions a lifelong program of learning by all, children and adults, in effective parenting (5). Burton White speaks of the need for professional educators who can teach parents how to educate their own children rather than for professional educators who can educate infants directly (6). Helen Beck would like to see neighborhood guidance centers where professional and neighborhood workers would be available for informal chats and education to prevent difficulties (7). Helen DeRosis advises that all appropriate educational facilities must undertake the task of parent education (8).

Those who support the need for parent education have few suggestions on funding sources. Governmental institutions "should" support such programs, but legislators are a long way from budgeting money since there is little general agreement on what is a "good" parent and what is the "ideal" child or adult. Also there is too little pressure from constituents, who are more concerned with treatment than prevention. Our best hope at this time appears to be the continued use of private and government funds to support research and demonstration projects.

Yet some form of educational effort is needed because:

Many parents are limiting the size of their families to one, two, or possibly three children.

These parents are concerned about doing a good job of rearing the children they choose to bring into the world.

More information is potentially available to parents today.

Extended family support systems are often miles away.

Family support systems in the community are usually out-of-date and do not incorporate results of research completed within the last 15 years.

Even middle class families do not automatically provide quality child care.

The middle class parent is looking for advice.

Three years ago, our daughter, a professor of educational psychology at Rutgers University, advised repeatedly that young couples having their first baby need someone to turn to for advice and empathy. At that time I was teaching child development to college students, and it seemed logical to offer the same information to parents outside of the college setting. Furthermore, it seemed that such services could be supported by payments from the parents themselves: after all, people pay for personal services from other professionals such as doctors, lawyers, and teachers.

Thus a private practice in parenting was born, and is now slowly developing. It is registered with the Texas Secretary of State as the "Positive Parenting Program" (PPP).sm

The PPP is organized around groups of parents who have or will have children of the same age; preferably the children are born within 30 days of each other. (With older children the groups have been kept within a 6 month age range, but this may prove to be too wide). Ideally, a group of 3 to 6 couples (spouses or the pregnant woman and a support person) begin to meet before delivery. We have tried to meet at least three times before delivery, in the 5th, 7th, and 8th month of pregnancy. This is designed to ameliorate some of the problems noted by Alice S. Rosse, i.e., that American couples begin parenthood with little preparation, limited learning during pregnancy, and few guidelines from society for successful parenthood, yet they must make an abrupt transition to 24 hour-a-day child care.

The goals of these first 1½ to 2 hour sessions are to develop knowledgeable, relaxed persons with realistic expectations for themselves and their babies. All meetings are held when both parents or two persons can attend (weekends or evenings). The parents already have excellent medical care and advice from their doctors. Through the PPP the parents also become acquainted with other community resources. Group support is provided to the parents in that I am available on the telephone day or night, and they have peers with whom they can compare notes and commiserate.

When the youngest baby in the group is about one month old we meet again. This is the most exciting meeting of all as parents enjoy seeing and hearing about each other's newborn babies. We meet again when the babies are three months old and then go on a regular three month schedule. In this way, child growth and development is approached in manageable stages. It is only practical to learn parenting step by small step. Group members are under no obligation to continue in the program, but since children constantly grow and change, a group once formed will continue to meet as long as three or more couples are interested. The three couple minimum is maintained for several reasons. This number of persons is required for dynamic group interaction, and we have found that social relationships develop best within groups which contain three or more couples. Also, as a purely practical consideration, a couple pays only a small fee for each session attended: a minimum group size is required to meet the expenses of the program.

The group concept has many advantages, the most important of which is that it creates a surrogate extended family. Specifically it offers three qualities of relationship that help alleviate the stress of parenting as outlined by Mary B. Lane (10) and T. Berry Brazelton (11): (1) the need to feel accepted as parents, (2) the need to identify with others who have like problems, and (3) the need for someone to listen with empathy.

Directors of parent-infant education in a similar program in the Seattle Community College district have noted beneficial effects when parents meet and share experiences (12). We have also noted that our sessions provide social contact, emotional support, and reassure parents that they are competent and their children are normal. A kind of intellectual stimulation occurs, much as when professional persons attend group meetings of colleagues (13). Parents sense that they too are growing as they encounter, share, and cope with common experiences of parenthood.

The director's role has remained flexible and is not rigidly defined. She must remain responsive to the needs of today's parents as persons, as spouses, and as citizens of the community. This may be in the capacity of listener, information giver, or resoutde locator. She acts as a facilitator who makes information available but does not advise or counsel parents how to use it. The parents must find their way with their unique set of resources and their own special baby.

Regular sessions are usually held at the Parent Learning Center, which is located in a comfortable, slightly old-fashioned house. For the first year the babies come with their parents; child care goes on without interrupting class activity. In fact, much of the enjoyment of the meetings comes from watching each other's babies grow. After the first year the infants are cared for by a sitter in another room of the building. The atmosphere of the sessions is that of parents and director participating in an endeavor where everyone teaches and everyone learns.

The format of the sessions is still evolving. Now each session is divided into 30 minutes of coffee and conversations, followed by 45 minutes of exchange of ideas and information, and 45 minutes of projection by the director as to the infant's probable growth and development during the next three months. In the group exchange, problems are discussed, potential solutions considered pro and con, and alternatives suggested by the director. Although the sessions are not structured for open-ended discussions of feelings or motives, the parents are encouraged to recall relevant memories from their own past. This reminds parents of their tendency to fall back on the way they were raised and makes the learning experience emotional as well as intellectual.

The curriculum for each session is based upon generally recognized key concepts. Various approaches and conflicting research conclusions are reported with references for further study. The following list of concepts is not exhaustive, but it exemplifies some of the basic material.

1. Drawing from Hugh W. Missildine (14), the Group for the Advancement of Psychiatry (15), Lee Salk (16) and others, the influence of one's own childhood on his parenting and the role of expectations for oneself and for one's child are examined.

2. Children are individuals influenced by inborn temperamental predispositions and differences in environment. Here we draw on the works of Chess, Thomas, and Birch (17), and T. Berry Brazelton (18).

3. Infants and children are strongly motivated to understand and act upon their world. There is an interchange between child and environment; the child is both influences by his world and in turn affects it (19).

4. Single parents and couples must learn that they need not feel alone in their parenting. Community resources can be mobilized to help them. Trusting relationships can be developed with a wide range of persons _other_ than family. From personal experiences and the insights of Mary Howell, we know that human support networks need not be based on family ties (20).

5. Attachment and separation experiences are anticipated and viewed as important episodes in the life of a child.

6. Insights from the works of Marshall H. Klaus and John H. Kennel regarding the importance of the first few minutes and hours after birth to parent bonding and later optimal development are discussed with parents before delivery (21).

7. Adults are important to children in all areas of development. Urie Bronfenbenner's views on the isolation of generations in our culture speaks to this situation (22).

8. Important characteristics of primary caregivers as described by Burton L. White are integrated into the curriculum (23).

The effectiveness of the program can only be measured at this time by the percentage of persons continuing in it. To date it is almost one hundred percent.

Dr. Kevin Swick asks, "Are parents an endangered species?" He answers in the affirmative - if we continue to force the total process of parenting on fathers and mothers. If, however, we develop teams including relatives, non-relatives, and citizens of the community, he feels that the outlook is more hopeful (24). The Positive Parenting Program^{sm} is one of many possible structures for teams whose parents is to surround each child with adults who will enjoy giving continuous, humane, and knowledgable care.

NOTE: Marion Pratt is director of the Positive Parenting Center in Ft. Worth, Texas.

REFERENCES

1. Michael Novak, "The Family Out of Favor," <u>Harpers</u>, April, 1976.

2. Group for the Advancement of Psychiatry, <u>The Joys and Sorrows of Parenthood</u>, New York, Charles Scribner's Sons, 1973.

3. Ibid.

4. The General Mills American Family Report, 1976-77, <u>Raising Children in a Changing Society</u>, Yankelovich, Skelly and White, Inc., Minneapolis, Minn., General Mills, Inc., 1977.

5. Ira J. Gordon, <u>The Infant Experience</u>, Columbus, Ohio, Charles E. Merrill Publishing Co., 1975.

6. Burton L. White, <u>The First Three Years of Life</u>, Englewood Cliffs, N.J., Prentice-Hall, Inc., 1975.

7. Helen L. Beck, <u>Don't Push Me I'm No Computer,</u> New York, McGraw-Hill Book Co., 1974.

8. Helen DeRosis, <u>Parent Power-Child Power</u>, New York, McGraw-Hill Book Co., 1974.

9. Alice S. Rossi, "Transition to Parenthood" in <u>Family In Transition</u>, Arlene S. Skolnick, Jerome H. Skolnick, Eds., Second Ed., Boston: Little, Brown, & Co., 1977.

10. Mary B. Lane, <u>Education for Parenting</u>, Washington, D.C. National Association for the Education of Young Children, 1975.

11. T. Berry Brazelton, <u>Infants and Mothers</u>, New York, Dell Publishing Co., Inc., 1969.

12. Lucile Charnley and Gloria Myre, "Parent-Infant Education," <u>Children Today</u>, March-April, 1977.

13. Ibid.

14. Hugh W. Missildine, <u>Your Inner Child of the Past</u>, New York, Simon and Schuster, 1963.

15. See note 2, supra.

16. Lee Salk, <u>Preparing for Parenthood</u>, New York, David McKay Company, Inc., 1974.

17. Stella Chess, Alexander Thomas, Herbert G. Birch, <u>Your Child is a Person</u>, New York: Viking Press, 1965.

18. See note 11, supra.

19. See e.g., Ira Gordon, <u>Human Development, A Transactional Perspective</u>, New York: Harper and Row Publishers, 1975.

20. Mary C. Howell, <u>Helping Ourselves: Families and the Human Network</u>, Boston: Beacon Press, 1975.

21. Marshall H. Klaus and John H. Kennell, <u>Maternal-Infant Bonding</u>, St. Louis: The C.V. Mosby Co., 1976.

22. Urie Bronfebrenner, "The Origins of Alienation," <u>Scientific American</u>, August, 1974.

23. Burtin L. White, Jean Carew Watts, <u>Experiences and Environment</u>, Englewood Cliffs, N.J., Prentice Hall, Inc., 1973.

24. Kevin J. Swick, "The Parenting Team: Concept, Process, Product," <u>Dimensions</u>, Journal of the Southern Association on Children Under Six, January 1978.

III

PROPOSED PRACTICES IN CAREGIVING

This section contains papers based on the idea that there are certain practices in caregiving that, not only need to continue, but need to do so with a vision that surpasses the existing bases. Rationales and statements indicating that the future of caregiving will need to come to terms with particular issues characterize the papers in this section.

INFANT STIMULATION PROGRAMS FOR THE HANDICAPPED: RATIONALE

by Mary Jane Gitter

We've come a long way, baby. In the last two decades, research on infancy has shown that infants, ages zero to three, possess more skills and capacities than previously imagined. Even as recently as the turn of the Twentieth Century, the infant was thought of as just a little bundle of mass confusion without any properly functioning senses; however, data collected since the early 1950's indicate that the infant is very capable of processing information from his outside world (Lewis, 1978).

Consequently, the infant's learning capacities have also undergone further scrutiny and evaluation. For instance, Siqueland (1968) and Bruner (1968) both report research where the sucking response was used to change the visual field by intensifying the illumination of a picture on a screen in one case and focusing a picture in the other. In both of these research cases, the infants demonstrated planned, intentional, organized, and sophisticated cognition.

Not surprisingly, the infant's social alertness is established also at an early age, such as in the recognition of their mother's voice and face. In fact, disruption of the mother's face-voice relationship results in distress in infants possibly even at one month of age (Lewis, 1978). Since the initiation of the infant to his world is through his social contacts, the role of the caregiver is obviously critical for the infant's emotional and intellectual development. The mother, for instance, serves as a loving caregiver who satisfies the infant's human drive for affection. The infant learns to recognize his mother's face and voice by frequent exposure to her. But what happens to the mother-child relationship in the case of an irritable deaf-blind baby, for instance, who cries easily and over reacts when he is handled? Isn't he likely to be left alone by his primary family caregivers? Could not a dynamic infant stimulation program "run defense" in such an instance?

It is also from the infant's social behavior - mother response that the infant learns the triggering effect of action on outcome. The infant who socially learns that one's actions have consequences, seems to develop motivation which is maintained even when tested in adulthood. Early feelings of competency may protect the child from later experiences with failure and enable the child to remain self-confident even though he had failed in the performance of some task (Lewis, 1978).

Conversely, early learned helplessness, a common pitfall for many handicapped infants, produces effects which are also expressed even in adulthood. Once learned, helplessness has a long-lasting effect. Perhaps the long-term effects of learned helplessness provide the best rationale for establishing infant stimulation programs for the handicapped. A handicapped infant is more prone to experience failure and to learn to be helpless because his possibly well-meaning but naive caregivers may tend to do everything for him. The continuing belief among the uninformed is that the infant is unsophisticated and unable to profit from experience. If early intervention can be provided both to infant *and* primary caregivers, surely these feelings of helplessness in the handicapped adult can be circumvented. The innocent ignorance of many primary caregivers is such an important variable to control for the future efficacy of their handicapped children's independence.

Luckily, most parents do not have to understand the intricacies of various learning theories which explain how their child learns. Children who are endowed with all the aptitudes, which we often take for granted, have a natural hunger for educational "discoveries".

On the other hand, retarded children have specific handicaps that reduce their ability to assimilate experiences. Because they have difficulty focusing their attention selectively, their cognitive development is slower and responses are grosser and more generalized. The basic premise of educational programs for infants is that therapists and teachers can help overcome these obstacles to learning from the very beginning and they can actualize the child's potential. An infant programmer will interact even with the fussy babies or the overly quiet and passive babies who might otherwise be left alone too frequently by their caregivers.

According to Marian Blackwell, a structured stimulation program may result in a variety of positive responses:

1. It gives tangible and rewarding ways for the entire family to relate with the infant.
2. Caregivers learn to notice and appreciate small improvements in the behavior of their child.
3. Structured stimulation heightens the child's level of attention.
4. It stimulates more specific, appropriate responses.
5. The child enjoys the enriched sensory environment.
6. A long-term association between the infant's family and community professionals is promoted.

Participation in a structured infant program is often exactly the "right dose of medicine" for the anxious parents of a handicapped newborn. As the child's deficits crystallize over time, many parents despair. While they may continue to clothe and feed the baby, they can become overwhelmed by the enormity of the child's handicapping problem. An active daily structured routine with clearly defined methods and goals can be a lifesaver psychologically for parent and child. A step-by-step program encourages parents to recognize the healthy aspects of their infant's behavior. When parents begin to feel competent in the total care of their handicapped child through the support of professionals, they experience genuine satisfaction because they know they are contributing all that is in their power to the future of their child's well-being.

Perhaps one of the most powerful examples of the potential advantageous effects of early intervention has been the shift in the adaptive behavior levels of children with Down's Syndrome. Five to ten years ago, textbooks classified most of these children as severely retarded; however, data from programs currently serving this population are indicating that most of these children are functioning within the mild to moderate range of retardation (Bricker, 1978). It is felt that earlier intervention has enhanced their learning potential.

There is also evidence from studies done by Frailberg in 1975 and Horton in 1976 that suggests deaf and blind children can make significant gains over non-intervention control groups if an early structured intervention program is implemented. Shearer and Shearer did research in 1976 that led to the conclusion that general stimulation programs for young significantly retarded children resulted in reliable gains following early intervention. They assessed the retardates on a variety of instruments such as the Bayley Scales of Infant Development. Baker and Heifetz in 1976 demonstrated that providing input to parents in terms of teaching them new management and instructional skills improves the performance of their children.

The research certainly seems to favor the development of infant stimulation programs, but what should be the goals of these programs? Dr. Bricker (1978), a researcher in early childhood, considers the following three dimensions as important goals:

1. Observable and measureable progress toward the acquisition of developmental milestones (e.g., crawling, walking, talking).

2. Growth of appropriate social behavior.

3. Intensified family involvement with the child's educational programming.

If we accept these as appropriate goals for most early intervention programs, how can we measure progress toward these goals?

Bricker (1978) suggests that the real measure of the success of a program will probably be in the answer to such questions as:

1. Were significantly fewer children in early intervention programs eventually admitted to institutions?

2. If the child was institutionalized, did the admission occur significantly later in life?

3. Did significantly fewer families suffer serious domestic complications (e.g., divorce, problems with other children in the family?)

If positive answers are given consistently over time to the aforementioned questions, then it would seem reasonable to suspect we have strong evidence of the successful impact of early intervention on the families of handicapped children.

The Outreach Program of Denton State School has several infant stimulation programs currently in our catchment area. Rather than limit ourselves solely to home visits, we usually have the infants come into our developmental centers regularly because we find:

1. It is more economical with regard to time and money for

our staff.
    2. Mothers then have an "excuse" to leave the house and commiserate with other parents with similar problems.
    3. Mothers have time for and interest in parent group meetings.
    4. The infant learns early to adapt to other caregivers and children.

There are certainly many ways to implement a delivery system for infant stimulation. We have also seen remarkable success with the infants receiving strictly homebound stimulation services. Despite whatever service delivery system you adopt, the primary concern for handicapped infants should be the earliest possible identification, assessment and program intervention. Early intervention does work!

NOTE: Mary Jane Gitter is director of the Outreach Program at the Denton State School, Denton, Texas.

REFERENCES

1. Baker, B. and Heifetz, L. The read project: Teaching manuals for parents of retarded children. Tjossem, T. (Ed.), Intervention Strategies for High Risk Infants and Young Children. Baltimore: University Park Press, 1976.

2. Bell, S.M. and Ainsworth, D. Infant crying and maternal responsiveness. Child Development, 43, 1171-1190, 1972.

3. Blackwell, M.V. Care of the Mentally Retarded. Boston: Little, Brown & Company, 1979.

4. Bricker, D. Early Intervention: The Criteria of Success. Drichta, C. (Ed.), Allied Health and Behavioral Sciences Volume I (2), 567-582, 1978.

5. Bricker, W. and Bricker, D. The Infant, toddler and preschool research and intervention project. Tjossem, T. (Ed.), Intervention Strategies with High Risk Infants and Young Children. Baltimore: University Park Press, 1976.

6. Bruner, J. Processes of Cognitive Growth: Infancy. (Volume III, Heinz Weiner Lecture Series.) Clark University Press with Bane Publishers, 1968.

7. Cliff, S., Gray, J., and Nymann, C. Mother Can Help. The El Paso Rehabilitation Center, 1974.

8. Fraiberg, S. Intervention in infancy: A program for blind infants. Frielander, B., Sterritt, G., and Kirk, G. (Eds.), Exceptional Infant Volume 3. New York: Bruner/Mazel, 1975.

9. Hannum, R.D., Rosellini, R.A., and Seligman, M.E.P. Learned helplessness in the rat: Retention and immunization. *Developmental Psychology*, 12 (5) 449-454, 1976.

10. Hanson, M. *Teaching Your Down's Syndrome Infant*. Baltimore: University Park Press, 1977.

11. Horton, K. Early intervention for hearing impaired infants and young children. Tjossem, T. (Ed.), *Intervention Strategies for High Risk Infants and Young Children*. Baltimore: University Park Press, 1976.

12. Lewis, M. and Goldberg, S. Perceptual - cognitive development in infancy: A generalized expectancy model as a function of the mother-child interaction. *Merrill-Palmer Quarterly*, 15 (1), 81-100, 1969.

13. Lewis, M. The Infant and Its Caregiver: The Role of Contingency. Drichta, C. (Ed.) *Allied Health & Behavioral Sciences Volume 1* (2), 469-492, 1978.

14. Shearer, D. and Shearer, M. The portage project: A model for early childhood intervention. Tjossem, T. (Ed.), *Intervention Strategies for High Risk Infants and Young Children*. Baltimore: University Park Press, 1976.

15. Siqueland, E.R. Conditioned sucking & visual reinforcers with human infants. Paper presented at Eastern Regional Meeting, Society for Research in Child Development, Worcester, Massachusetts, April, 1968.

RECREATION AND LEISURE PROGRAMMING IN
CAREGIVING FOR THE HANDICAPPED

by Claudine Sherrill

We are all functioning at a small fraction of our capacity to live fully in its total meaning of loving, caring, creating, and adventuring. Consequently, the actualizing of our potential can become the most exciting adventure of our lifetime.
Herbert Otto

Helping persons who are ill, disabled, or handicapped is self-actualizing. It brings new dimensions to loving, caring, creating, and adventuring. It presents new vistas in the use of leisure, ours and theirs. For most of us, caregiving is a leisure time activity, an act of volunteerism, a reflection of values.

The purpose of this paper is to issue a challenge... a dare to be different from most Americans in our use of leisure time, an invitation to explore the meanings of humanism, a call to improve our quality of life. How do most Americans spend their leisure? In the early 1950s Jay B. Nash, a philosopher in recreation and leisure services, wrote:

On all sides there are glaring indications that, given leisure, man will become a listener, a watcher, a sitter. He will become a victim of spectatoritis, a blanket description to cover all kinds of passive amusement entered into merely to escape boredom.

Use of Leisure In America

Technological advances have indeed given us more leisure during these past thirty years. What are we doing with it? According to a 1979 survey by pollster Louis Harris, 84 percent of 1,442 adults questionned nationwide named eating as their top leisure-time activity (NRPA, p. 3). The next four most frequently mentioned leisure time pursuits were watching television, 41 percent; listening to radio, 40 percent; reading, 39 percent; listening to music at home, 39 percent. It seems that Jay B. Nash's prediction is becoming increasingly true; most Americans are listeners, watchers, sitters.

Other leisure activities reported in the Harris poll include the following; (1) 36 percent frequently spend time fixing things around the house; (2) 25 percent report social activities like dining out, going dancing, and giving or attending parties; (3) 25 percent report they frequently spend their leisure-time having sex; and (4) 23 percent spend their leisure-time deeply involved in church or club activities. Twenty-one percent devote much of their leisure time to such outdoor activities as hiking, fishing, hunting, and boating. Only 20 percent reported spending a lot of time on hobbies or specialized pursuits, and only 19 percent indicated frequent participation in sports.

It appears that for most of us quality of life can be improved by changing our leisure life styles, by reaching out for divergent experiences, and by interacting with new persons. Each of us can be the master of his/her own destiny; we can set goals, change our behaviors, and enter into new relationships. The ease with which we expand our lives relates largely to self-concept. Combs, et. al. (1971, p. 156) state in this regard:

> Persons with high self-esteem, able to accept themselves, are also able to accept other people; this makes effective interaction with others much more likely. Because they believe in and trust themselves, they can act with high degrees of autonomy. They are freewheelers and able to move off in new directions, which is what is meant by creativity. People open to new experience enjoy exploring...

<u>Needs of Handicapped In Relation to Leisure</u>

Handicapped persons, like us, have the same needs for loving, caring, creating, and adventuring. Unlike us, however, the 10-12 percent of our population which is ill, disabled, or handicapped has an abundance of free, unoccupied time. What are some of the facts that document their special need for leisure/recreation education?

Razeghi and Davis (1979, p. 356) report that 40 percent of all disabled adults are employed as compared with 74 percent of the nondisabled. Moreover the United States Census statistics show that 85 percent of the disabled have annual incomes of less than $7000. Of these, 52 percent make less than $2000 a year.

The handicapping condition with the greatest incidence in this country is mild/moderate mental retardation. Employment statistics for this group show that only 21 percent are fully employed after high school, 40 percent are underemployed, and 26 percent remain unemployed (Hightower, 1975). Research shows that mentally retarded persons can work successfully in a number of salaried jobs. It is a known fact, however, that employers typically give jobs to the applicants with the best credentials, not only in work skills, but also in attractiveness, personableness, and intelligence. Good vocational education does not solve employment problems when work opportunities are few and/or nonexistent.

What do the underemployed and the unemployed do with their abundance of free time. Edgerton (1967) offers anecdotes describing the recreation/leisure practices of several mentally retarded persons. Illustrative of these are the following:

Lulu Age: 30 IQ: 48 Discharge: 1956 Single

Her spare time is usually spent in her room watching
TV or looking at magazines, mostly pictorial ones.
Perhaps once every six weeks she goes to a nearby
movie, and on Sundays she likes to get on a bus, ride
to the end of the line, and come back again. She
enjoys talking to anyone who will listen, but television is her great passion. She watches a variety
of programs avoiding only "the heavy or sad ones."
She says fervently, "I just don't know what I'd do
without TV. It's my only friend."

Walter Age: 20 IQ: 61 Discharge: 1958 Single

He sometimes watches TV at home with his parents, but
he finds life at home so unpleasant that "I got to get
out with the boys." He devotes himself to a masquerade
as a delinquent teen-ager by following normal teen-agers about and hoping for acceptance. He tries to
talk to them of cars, music, girls, drinking, and
fighting, but they consistently ignore or insult him.
Nevertheless, his activities continue to center upon
efforts to be accepted as a normal teen-ager. When
he has some money, he can buy a moment's contact with
this teen-age world, but never becomes a participant
in it.

Jose (Mexican-American) Age: 34 IQ: 48 Discharge: 1957 Single

He loves to talk to friends, "tease" girls, and simply
enjoy his freedom. "I just walk wherever I want to go,
like a free bird." His only regular pastimes are drinking
beer and an occasional visit to a thirty-five-cent movie
on skid row. Of course, most of his time is leisure
time, and one of his favorite time-consumers is sleep:
"I love to sleep. I sleep almost all the time, it seems
like."

Myrtle Age: 31 IQ: 56 Discharge: 1958 Married

Her leisure is spent entirely with her husband. They
stay home together, talk, and watch TV. They used to
attend social meetings of "a handicapped persons club"
(he is paraplegic) but they no longer do so. Except
on Sundays when they attend church, they rarely leave
the house other than to shop: "We just stay home and
talk and enjoy things."

In conclusion Edgerton (p. 127) states:

A consideration of the uses of leisure time is critically instructive because better than anything else available to us, the use of leisure serves to indicate the richness or impoverishment in the lives of these retarded persons... The basic leisure-time pattern for the ex-patients is a combination of conversation and television.

Research Findings On the Handicapped

Clearly caregiving services for the handicapped should include recreation and leisure programming designed to enhance their understanding of alternatives in the use of leisure. In this regard, the handicapped are probably little different from the rest of us. Remember the findings of the 1979 Harris poll: 84 percent of the adults interviewed named eating as their top leisure activity. Sherrill and Ruda (1977, p. 33) reported the leisure preferences of 40 retarded men, ages 18-33, in a halfway house in Denton. Activities checked as preferred by 90 percent or more of the subjects included barbecues, camping, riding in cars, picnics, collecting addresses, cooking, ice cream and snacks, radio listening, record listening, and television. Four of these ten preferences focused on eating! How similar we really are!

Research shows that loneliness, alienation, and transportation problems act as major barriers in recreation participation for the handicapped (Noe, 1977). Stanfield's (1973) study is most often cited in this regard. Interviews with parents of 120 former students of special education study of 27 mentally retarded men, ages 19-36, who were living in a community-based residential facility. Almost all of the subjects ranked community-based recreation activities higher than those done in the dormitory. In rank order from high to low, their preferences were bowling, movies, dancing, picnics, cooking, camping, and basketball.

In most instances, however, the discrepancy between leisure preferences and practices are great. Unlike you and me, the handicapped seldom have control over their own lives and leisure (Dixon, 1978); they seldom have the skills and/or the money to use public transportation; and those who live at home infrequently have friends with whom to share recreational pursuits.

Trend Toward Listening To The Handicapped

The importance of listening to the handicapped and of facilitating their self direction is gaining increasing recognition as a goal of caregiving. Sherrill and Ruda (1977) state in this regard:

...recreation programming...must evolve from the clients themselves. It must be individualized and nurtured by a recreation professional who views himself as a facilitator of learning. Most important, the learning experiences in recreation should focus not on skills but upon the humanistic qualities that underlie man's need to

> aspire, to dream, to value, and to cherish. Without
> these qualities, leisure has little meaning...

Illustrative of the new emphasis on listening to the handicapped classes revealed that most of these persons, now ages 19-21, spent their time at home engaging in such solitary activities as watching television, listening to the radio or record player, and looking at books and magazines. Only 23 percent of these young persons felt they had friends that they could go and visit, and only 60 percent had sufficient skills to travel about their community unchaperoned. Think what our lives would be if we had no friends to visit and lacked the skills to get out of the house and go places to make new acquaintances. Surely caregiving includes the facilitation of friendships.

Katz and Yekutiel (1974) report similar findings in Israel after interviewing parents of 178 retarded adults, ages 17-50, with intelligence quotients of 31 to 84. The two main problems identified regarding leisure time use were the lack of suitable companions and the lack of proper facilities. The most often reported type of leisure activity was listening to the radio or watching television. Only 22 percent reported that they had friends and engaged in social interaction outside their family. Katz and Yekutiel concluded that the vocational training of these persons seemed to have been successful but the training for social and leisure time was obviously inadequate.

Sherrill and Iwanski (1977) reported an indepth are the May 1977, first national White House Conference on Handicapped Individuals, held in Washington, D.C. and the May 1979, national conference entitled: "The Consumer Speaks: An Evaluation of Physical Education, Recreation, and Sports by People With Special Needs", held in Nashville, Tennessee. The reports of these conferences cite recommendations/resolutions with strong implications for caregiving.

The year 1981 has been designated as the "International Year of the Disabled". Through interacting with the ill, the disabled, and the handicapped, we gain new insights into caregiving as well as caring, loving, creating, and adventuring. Indeed we become more human. Mayeroff proposes that <u>caring</u> is the quality most central to humanism. The following lines from his beautiful book entitled ON CARING seem appropriate to end these thoughts on recreation and leisure programming in caregiving for the handicapped:

> In the context of a man's life, caring has a way of
> ordering his other values and activities around it.
> When this ordering is comprehensive, because of the
> inclusiveness of his carings, there is a basic stabil-
> ity in his life; he is "in place" in the world, instead
> of being out of place, or merely drifting or endlessly
> seeking his place. Through caring for certain others,
> by serving them through caring, a man lives the meaning

of his own life. In the sense in which a man can ever
be said to be at home in the world, he is at home not
through dominating, or explaining, or appreciating,
but through caring and being cared for.

Mayeroff's book should be read by every caregiver who resolves to develop further the human qualities of caring, prizing, trusting, and respecting self as well as others.

NOTE: Claudine Sherrill is a faculty member in the Department of Physical Education at the Texas Woman's University at Denton.

REFERENCES

1. Combs, Arthur; Avila, Donald; Purkey, William. *Helping Relationships: Basic Concepts for the Helping Professions*. Boston: Allyn and Bacon, Inc., 1971.

2. "Cooperation Unity Prevails In Consumer Conference." *IRUC Briefings*. May 1979.

3. Dixon, Jess. "Expanding Individual Control In Leisure Participation While Enlarging the Concept of Normalcy." *Therapeutic Recreation Journal*. 12, 3 (Third Quarter 1978): pp. 20-24.

4. Edgerton, Robert. *The Cloak of Competence: Stigma in the Lives of the Mentally Retarded*. Berkeley: University of California Press, 1967.

5. "Harris Survey." *Dateline: NRPA*. 2,3 April-May 1979.

6. Katz, Shlomo and Yekutiel, Esther. "Leisure Time Problems of Mentally Retarded Graduates of Training Programs." *Mental Retardation*. 12 (June 1974): pp. 54-57.

7. Hightower, Mae D. "Status Quo Is Certain Death." *Journal of Rehabilitation*. 42, 2 (April 1976): pp. 32-35.

8. Mayeroff, Milton. *On Caring*. New York: Harper and Row, 1971.

9. Nash, Jay B. *Philosophy of Recreation and Leisure*. St. Louis: The C.V. Mosby Company, 1953.

10. Noe, F.P. "Effects of Transportation and Alienation as Barriers to Recreation Participation for the Inner City Disabled." *Therapeutic Recreation Journal*. 11, 2 (Second Quarter, 1977): 74-80.

11. Razeghi, Jane and Davis, Sharon. "Federal Mandates for the Handicapped: Vocational Education Opportunity and Employment." *Exceptional Children*. 45, 5 (February 1979): pp: 353-359.

12. Sherrill, Claudine and Iwanski, Ruth Ann. "Self Concepts and Leisure Preferences of Mentally Retarded Adult Men." *Therapeutic Recreation Journal*. 11, 1 (First Quarter, 1977): pp. 23-27.

13. Sherrill, Claudine and Ruda, Lucy. "A Time To Listen." *Parks and Recreation*. 12, 11 (November 1977): pp. 30-33.

14. Stanfield, James. "What Happens to the Retarded Child When He Grows Up?" *Exceptional Children*. 39 (April 1973): 548-552.

15. White House Conference on Handicapped Individuals. *Volume Three: Implementation Plan*. Washington, D.C.: U.S. Government Printing Office, 1978.

PROVIDING EFFECTIVE CARE FOR THE AGED

by Cora Martin

I am delighted to have been asked to participate in your conference today. I regret to say that it is still the exception, rather than the rule, for the aging client to be recognized in a conference such as this. Your conference organizers are to be congratulated - and thanked - for the aged are a group that we all can look forward to joining, some of us sooner than others.

Someone has said that "every man would live long, but none would grow old." Yet we do grow old, and living long almost inevitably brings on physical, psychological, and social changes which make it more probable that the aged will be the recipients of some type of care.

The proportion of the aged in the population of the United States has increased from 4% in 1900 to 10% in 1975, and we have begun to differentiate three groups of "old people" (since the age span is at least 20 years - from 65 to 85). Those from 65 to 74 mostly are in good health, financially better off, and better educated than the older cohorts. They are the _go-go aged_. Those from 75 to 84, the _go-slow aged_, begin to accumulate physical problems and often to lose social support. Those 85+ are the _no-go aged_. One way to substantiate this is by looking at the figures for institutionalization in nursing homes or personal care homes. Between the ages of 65 and 74 there are only 12 admissions per thousand per year in the population. For those 75 to 84 the rate rises to 52/1000, and for those 85+ it is 203/1000 - roughly one in five.[1]

This is the picture at the present time. The age structure of the country is changing, and by the year 2000 12.5% of the population will be over 65.[2] When the baby-boom cohort reaches the age of 64 - around 2010 - we will see a major increase in the proportion and the number of those 65+. If fertility rates remain lower than replacement, or barely at replacement levels, the proportion of aged individuals in the population could grow precipitously. Do you remember the way schools had to be built for the baby-boom youngsters when they reached school age? In a few years we will have to begin preparing for this cohort to have new services and in general for their impact on the social structure.

Nor is the growth confined to the _go-go_ or young-old. In 1950 persons 80 years of age and older constituted 14% of those over 65; by 1975 this proportion had increased to 20%, and it is expected to continue to increase.[3] In fact, individuals over 80 are the fastest growing part of the whole population structure.

I hope that I haven't completely put you to sleep with these statistics, but I also hope that I have shown you something of the dimensions of need for effective care that exists now and alerted you to the fact that the need will grow.

Robert Butler, head of the National Institute on Aging, wrote a book in 1975 which won the Pulitzer Prize for that year. It was titled <u>Why Survive? Being Old in America</u>. In it Butler maintains that the question "Why Survive?" is real and challenges our society to improve attitudes, opportunities, and services to the old in America.

Louis Lowy contends that "The presence of older people poses new demands on all of us. We must reconceptualize the life cycle and our accustomed modes of thinking about the distribution of work and play, the uses of time throughout life, the relationships between three and four generations of family members, and their new statuses and roles."[4] Years ago Juanita Kreps expounded the thesis that our present arrangement of 25 years of preparation for work, 40 years of work, and 20-25 years of leisure was in need of some careful rethinking. She threw out the suggestion of multiple careers, multiple preparation periods for those careers, and multiple leisure periods. It sounds like a winner to me! At no time in our history have we had as many three- and four-generation families as we have now. The roles of parent, child, and grandchild are undergoing redefinition as they pertain to the last part of the life cycle. Many "children," responsible for the care of their now <u>no-go</u> parents, are themselves in their 60s. The grandchildren are 40. Greatgrandchildren are probably in their 20s. Contrary to the myth that older people "used to be taken care of" by their families, there is probably more interaction and care-giving now than at any time in the past.

Work with the aging is a challenge - an exciting challenge - to practitioners in a wide variety of professions: medicine, social work, policy formulation and administration, recreation and leisure, nutrition, nursing, physical therapy, occupational therapy, libraries, and, not least, education, for the old are engaging in education activities in increasing numbers.

In education for the professions we are slow to realize the potential. For example, I've been working with medical schools and although more than half of the average general practitioner's caseload is going to be composed of those over 65 (since they have accumulated more "insults of aging") only a small number of medical schools have special courses, or sequences, or practicums in aging. Yet no medical school in the United States fails to have pediatrics. The social work caseload of those working for the department of human resources is likely to be heavily weighted with old-old, but most schools of social work have very little in their curriculum which provides didactic material on the aging process, the physical problems of aging, etc. I could go on and on. The faculties of the schools of the so-called "helping professions" have not waked up or are just now waking up to the changing demographic picture in America.

I submit that the first, and most effective, thing that we can do to provide effective care for the aged is to advocate for change in the professional curricula. There should be a course on aging in every school, and other part of the curriculum should also sensitize budding practitioners to the challenges of working with the aged. Practical experiences must be provided so that the novice-professionals can have some hands-on experience with older people and discover for themselves the delight of working with clients who can bring the past to life as they relive the Depression, World War II, or other great societal upheavals that the young have only heard about. They can observe the tremendous variation in the old - after all, they have had three-quarters of a century or more to develop individuality! We at the Center for Studies in Aging have seen that "aging" is a subject which "turns on" many young people.

A second way to improve care of the aged is to include information about aging in the continuing education/in-service education programs of professionals. The subject-matter on aging is of inherent interest to most of them; with this knowledge many of their clients can be dealt with more effectively. In addition, the knowledge is often helpful in their personal lives and they welcome the opportunity to learn more.

Finally, we can all - in whatever professional capacity we serve - work toward an integration of the care system. This is not a problem that is unique to aging clients. Fragmentation bedevils all of us who are concerned with care-giving. I submit that it is particularly damaging in trying to secure effective care for the aging; their limited mobility, sensory deficits, frequent poverty, and, in many instances, little education all make fragmentation of services particularly trying for the aged.

To conclude my remarks I would like to call your attention to the changing character of the aged. Older people in the future will be better educated and healthier because they had better access to improved health care, nutrition and housing. They will therefore have higher expectations in terms of health care, living facilities, and other amenities. Retirement will have been expected and planned for. Further, they will have learned how to use the political system to their advantage. The helping professions must be aware of this. We are going to expect great things from you.

NOTE: Cora Martin is co-director of the Center for Studies in Aging at North Texas State University, Denton, Texas.

REFERENCES

1. Ward, Russell. *The Aging Experience*, J.B. Lippincott Co., New York, 1979, p. 388.

2. Ibid., p. 27

3. Ibid.

4. Lowy, Louis. *Social Work with the Aging*, Harper & Row, New York, 1979, p. xiii.

IV

SPECIFIC CONCERNS IN CAREGIVING

The focus of this section is on the problems and practices of caregivers who face particular types of situations. It must be emphasized that each caregiving situation is special and it is not the intention of the authors to lessen the importance of this statement by presenting information on particular situations. It is hoped that the focused approach will enable the reader to see philosophies of caregiving put into practice.

PROMOTING PRO-SOCIAL BEHAVIOR IN CHILDREN

by Frank Vitro

Introduction

Parents, teachers, clerics and a variety of other helping professions have a common mission of promoting behavior that is beneficial to society. Most youngsters learn quite early in their development that it is desirable to share and cooperate with others and to help and comfort others whenever possible. This behavior, which is assumed to emerge at some point during the pre-school and primary school years is referred to as prosocial behavior since it promotes positive social interactions. Pro-social behavior specifically refers to actions that result in benefit or assistance to others without expectation of external rewards or anticipation of other forms of retribution. Pro-social behavior reflects behavior that is considered moral or ethical by one's cultural standards (e.g., generosity, sharing, altruism, empathy, cooperation, helpfulness, honesty, etc.). Participation in activities designed to improve the general welfare of society by the reduction of social injustices, inequities and violence are also considered pro-social as they are not only beneficial to individual recipients but also are considered to be ingrained in the "moral fiber" of society.

Proscriptive vs. Prescriptive Child Rearing Practices

Most people take it for granted that morality training is simply a matter of teaching youngsters what not to do. At home and at school we forever admonish, scold, and warn children about the consequences of violating a prohibition or rule. This is what I refer to as proscriptive discipline. This approach attempts to transmit morality or standards of behavior by identifying and prohibiting unacceptable or anti-social forms of behavior and then establishing appropriate sanctions and/or punishments for such behaviors. That is, most people tend to point out the don'ts or thou shalt nots and moralize upon the consequences of doing wrong, rather than to emphasize the merits or benefits of doing right. This philosophy is epitomized by the ever-increasing demands made by the public that our law enforcement agencies become more effective (proscriptive); that our judicial system become more punitive and expedient in the administration of justice (proscriptive); that our prison facilities improve their security conditions (proscriptive); and a host of other reforms sought in the name of reducing crime and its social concimittants. However, these have been and will remain only stop-gap measures and "band-aid" strategies that deal with only the surface symptoms of a more deeply rooted pathology.

The problem stems from not only the child learning antisocial and maladaptive behaviors but also from his failure to learn effective socialization skills and pro-social behavior. In our child-rearing practices we generally tend to overdo the "thou shalt nots", and the transgressions to be avoided and the prohibited areas of human behavior. From early toddler stages the child hears, "don't be naughty," "don't hit your sister," "don't make a mess," "don't lie," etc. Such admonitions rely heavily on the arousal of unpleasant internalized guilt or anxiety reactions to inhibit or curtail the violation of prohibited behaviors. There is ample evidence to support the presence of this prevalent negativistic approach to child-rearing. I recently conducted a survey among over 200 elementary school children (first and second and third graders). I simply asked two questions:

1. What are some of the bad or naughty things that people sometimes do? (e.g., steal, fight, lie). Try to think of as many of these as you can in 2 minutes.
2. What are some of the good or nice things that people sometimes do? (e.g., share, help, cooperate). Try to think of as many of these as you can in 2 minutes.

The results clearly showed that youngsters tend to be far more aware of the bad or prohibited behaviors than they are of the desirable of pro-social behaviors. When the predominant message of disciplinary child-rearing practices is "don't do these things" instead of "learn to do these things" the child will typically incorporate such prohibitions as his/her primary code of morality and thus be more aware of the "don't" rather than the "do."

 A. <u>Interpersonal (Social Competencies)</u>
  1. <u>Altruism</u>
   a. Empathy (understanding and feeling for others). Social perspective sharing.
   b. Charitability or generosity-giving material and/or assistance to others.
   c. Sharing.
   d. Cooperation.
  2. <u>Communication</u>
   a. Listening skills.
   b. Interpretation skills.
   c. Expressive skills-verbal-non-verbal.
  3. <u>Role-Introjection</u> (role-playing)
 B. <u>Cognitive (Intellectual) Competencies</u>
  1. <u>Perceptual attentiveness and concentration</u>
   (focusing) e.g., awareness of rules or rights of others.
  2. <u>Perceptual Objectivity</u> (accuracy and truth in interpretation or reality, contributes to honesty)
  3. <u>Reasoning and Judgement Skills</u>
   a. Logical thinking skills.
   b. Inductive vs. deductive skills.
   c. Rational problem-solving skills.
  4. <u>Decision-making Skills</u>

C. Civic and Societal Competencies
  1. Understanding of and respect for law and order.
  2. Awareness of and respect for the rights and properties of others.
  3. Understanding of the concept of justice as applied to our society.
  4. Understanding and acceptance of civic responsibilities (voting, tax paying, serving in elective office, etc.).

As you can see in this model, the true confirmation of morality lies in the quality of interpersonal relationships that are established among people. Prosocial behavior and moral conduct is the type of behavior which enables people to experience greater trust in and appreciation for others, increased cooperation, reduced social distance, and sense of self-respect and personal harmony.

A Prescriptive-Inductive Approach to Pro-Social Training

Why not reverse the situation and use more techniques that evoke pleasant internalized feelings or reactions such as pride or self-esteem to promote desirable behavior? We tend to overlook the value of prescriptive or pro-social training strategies where the emphasis is on what to do, not what should not be done.

I propose that specific categories of prosocial skills can be taught through inductive training techniques. There are clearly definable competencies that can be nurtured and promoted at home and at school. The following model represents an attempt to develop a pro-social approach to morality training. Specific techniques and activities to be used will be spelled out in a later paper, but generally, methods include inductive reasoning, modeling and role-playing, values clarification exercises, and self-analysis activities. It will be noted that this prescriptive approach emphasizes positive, prosocial and desirable skills to be learned by the learner and as such might be called a pro-active rather than a reactive approach to morality and socialization training.

Dimensions of Pro-Social Behavior
  A. Personal Competencies
    1. Self-regulatory Behavior
       a. Self-restraint-control or management of aggression or other destructive impulses; patience; self-control.
       b. Delay or postponement of gratification (resistance to temptation).
       c. Tolerance of frustration and unpreventable discomfort.
       d. Acceptance of responsibility and commitments.
    2. Self-understanding
       a. Objective self-analysis and self-disclosure (ability to clearly and objectively understand oneself).
       b. Self-appreciation and acceptance.
       c. Career and other role-identity awareness.

       d. Emotional awareness-understanding and coping with fear, hate, joy, sadness, love, shame, etc.
3. <u>Self-assertion</u> (volition).
    a. Goal setting.
    b. Persistence.

In conclusion, the importance of this area of psychological research is underscored by the fact that it relates to nothing less than the quality of human existence. Particularly in today's society when there appears to be a rise in violence, injustice, and inhumanities. Improvement of the human condition must, more than ever before, become the primary mission of psychology, particularly of the fields of developmental and social psychology. The accomplishment of this goal will be contingent upon the improvement and intensification of research and inquiry into the development and promotion of pro-social behavior.

NOTE: Frank Vitro is on the faculty at Texas Woman's University at Denton, in the Department of Psychology and Philosophy.

THE CULTURAL-LINGUISTIC DIFFERENCES OF BILINGUAL CHILDREN

by Ysau N. Flores, Jr.

At any given school day, approximately two million children in the United States do not go to school. Some do not go because they are ill-fed or ill-clothed. Some do not go because they might have handicaps far worse than a language one. Some do not go because they do not speak the language in their classroom and they are embarrassed. They have been subjected to ridicule.

If a non-English speaking child comes to school and the child's ability is such that he/she cannot benefit from the school's program, he may be told: "child, you change; we will not change the program." The now famous 1974 Bilingual Education U.S. Supreme Court Lau vs. Nichols case reversed this development.

Millions of dollars are being spent each fiscal year on innovative programs designed to improve the education of minority children in our schools, but most of these special programs will continue to be ineffective until their crucial inadequacy has been recognized and corrected. Richard Light, formerly of the U.S. Office of Education and now with the State University of New York, pointed out the shocking lack of understanding of cultural and linguistic differences that is responsible for the failure of a number of these programs. The inadequate preparation of teachers and administrators to understand and serve the critical needs of children from different cultural and linguistic backgrounds is appalling. Viable teacher training institutions and pre/inservice programs must provide the following: courses in linguistic and anthropology; methodology of second language acquisition; and techniques of teaching second language learning. This type of program is necessary if bilingual education teachers are to acquire the necessary "caregiving" skills for working effectively with children whose language and culture differ from the mainstream.

Educators who are not native English speakers have misgivings about their linguistic competence. Native English speakers who do not know the language of their students wonder whether they can teach effectively. Educators everywhere are uneasy about controversies over current linguistic theories and about the realistic contributions linguistics, psycholinguistics, or other sciences can make to language learning and teaching. They are deeply concerned about keeping abreast of the "best, most modern" methods of teaching, about the attention being given in the literature to individualized instruction, and to performance objectives. They are equally concerned about tests, grades, homework, uninterested students, and linguistically-culturally different pupils. Many of these concerned educators are strikingly similar in that they want to become more effective educators. Non-native and native English speakers alike express hope that they can develop communicative competence in their pupils despite what some consider to be their own linguistic limitations. These educators want to motivate their students so that they will find language learning a pleasurable, successful activity. These educators are aware of the fact that they can help their students and their community by providing another medium by which to communicate.

Bilingual education is a unique art of caregiving. It involves the use of two languages as the medium of instruction in part or in all of the curriculum. Bilingual education may be one-way or two-way. In two-way bilingual education, children in each ethnic and linguistic group learn curricula through their own language and through a second language. All curricula may be taught in both languages to both groups. Two-way bilingual education means that one takes the "best of both worlds," that is, the child receives instruction in both the native and dominant language.

School districts do not purposely deny children education. If, however, a school district is providing a product, and that product is education, the consumers (children) should not be forced to change in response to the product by giving up their native language. The product (education) must change to accomodate the needs and abilities of the consumers.

NOTE: Ysau N. Flores, Jr. is a consultant in bilingual education with Region XI Education Service Center, Ft. Worth, Texas.

REFERENCES

1. Abrahams, Roger D. and Rudolph C. Troike. *Language and Cultural Diversity in American Education*. New Jersey: Prentice-Hall, Inc., 1972.

2. Cohen, A.D. *A Sociolinguistic Approach to Bilingual Education*. Boston: Newbury House Publishers, Inc., 1975.

3. Finocchiaro, M. *English as a Second Language: From Theory to Practice*. New York: Regents Publishing Co., Inc., 1974.

4. Steinman, E. "Rights of Children to an Equal Education Opportunity: The Lau Mandate." San Antonio, Texas, April, 1979.

RANDY: AN ALLERGIC CHILD WITH READING PROBLEMS

by Doylene R. Hogg

The story of Randy is not too unusual. You can see other students, like Randy in special education resource rooms across the country. Medical authorities might point out that the signs of Randy's problems were there all along, but at the time we were going through this, no one offered this solution to the problem. I do not pretend to know all there is about allergies, but if by reading this story it will cause you to stop and think about the children you see, it may help them.

It was a cold and foggy night on January 5, when Randy chose to enter this world. He was beautiful, healthy (or least he seemed to be) and weighed almost 8 pounds. This was our second child. We took him home with all the hopes, dreams, and plans - and I might add ignorance - a young couple could have. He was a good baby. He ate well and slept all night after the first week.

About the third week in his life trouble came for the first time. Randy began to throw up his milk. He lost weight and cried much of the time. The doctor changed his formula. We would try one formula for a week and if there was no improvement, we would change to another one. This went on for several weeks. Each time Randy would take the new formula without any problems, then the same problems would begin again.

When he was about 3 months old the doctor sent us to the hospital to have Randy X-rayed. The doctors were concerned about an obstruction in the stomach or small intestines. The X-ray showed nothing.

We had used all of the formulas on the market except one made from soybeans. When he tried this, it worked. Randy grew on a normal basis from that point on. There were no noticable reactions to any other foods at that time.

As Randy grew older, I began to notice that he had to eat on a very regular basis. If we were late with a meal, he would grow weak, and become very faint. We found that if we would give him something to eat or drink, especially something sweet, he would appear better. Then he had to have something more substantial, like meat or cheese, then in about an hour he would be back to normal. This condition grew worse as he grew older and would hurry through meals or skip a meal to do something special. Also, he would eat junk food instead of a meal. This caused some very frightening incidents. His doctor ran a blood sugar level test on him and we were told that Randy was hypoglycemic. He was placed on a high protein diet - complete with six meals a day. Randy functioned very well, for a while, on this diet.

One summer day we went to a peach orchard to gather some peaches.

We had not been there long, when Randy began to cry. When I looked around I could not believe what I was seeing. Randy had turned red and was beginning to swell. His face had few features left. There was an old man working in the orchard, he grabbed Randy and ran to an old hand pump well. He held Randy under the spout and began to pump. This was a deep well, with clear, cold water. The man kept holding Randy under the flowing cold water until there seemed to be some relief. Then I put Randy into the car, with the air conditioning on and took him home. The redness and swelling left almost as fast as it came. From that day on, Randy could no longer touch a peach. He can eat one, if someone will peel it for him, but if he touches the fuzz on the skin, he has the same reaction.

Every year at Christmas time, Randy was always sick. Twice the doctor thought he had the Chicken Pox. But after two weeks and no change, we were told it was not the Chicken Pox but probably some allergy. This was the first time this word was used to diagnose any of the problems that Randy had. We did not know what the cause could be since it would go away in the same mysterious way that it came. Then, one year we were getting ready for Christmas. We went to the farm and gathered some cedar branches and red berries and leaves. On the way home, Randy broke out with the Chicken Pox-like bumps. When we took the cedar out of the car and he was not exposed to it, the bumps went away. We bought an artificial tree and never had that problem again.

These were unrelated events and seemed not to be connected in any way. But as time went on, we were to learn the basic and universal connection of all these things. In the first 5 years of his life, Randy had grown into a big, strong boy, with a very happy outlook on life. He seemed to be quick to learn during this time. He loved to listen to his favorite books being read aloud to him. The medical quirks that happened to my son all seemed to be separate and not joined by any common bond or connection. By the use of avoidance, we continued on with life in as normal a way as possible. He was affectionate and did not cause much trouble. He would play very intently, either with other children or by himself. He always seemed to be happy.

The time came for Randy to start school. He was looking forward to it, but like most 6 year-olds, felt a little insecure about leaving home. His sister was in the fourth grade and school was a very positive experience for her. He judged school by some of her comments. If she was excited, he would be excited too. If she complained, then he worried that something like that might happen to him.

Once he actually got started, he really liked school and looked forward to going everyday. About half way through the first grade there was evidence that something was wrong. Randy did not learn to read. In fact, he had great difficulty distinguishing one letter from another. I talked to the teachers and the principal about repeating the first grade, but they said that sometimes boys lag a little in the first grade and will make up for it later.

By the time Randy reached the third grade, the whole problem looked pretty bad. He still was not reading and still had difficulty with the different letters. Especially the look-a-likes; bd, gpq, mw, sz. Words like "was" and "saw" were the same to him. He would come home very discouraged. Sometimes there would be stacks of homework for him to do. He would work from the time he came in until time to go to bed. Many times that was not enough to finish all the work he had to do. It was very hard for him to read the material, then work out the problems. Sometimes the whole family would get involved in trying to help him with his homework. Many times he would rather take a zero on a paper instead of struggling all night with it.

This attitude became worse as time went on. Finally, my husband and I requested that Randy be tested, to see if he would qualify for Special Education or any other help available. The tests were given to him. His I.Q. was in the bright normal limits, according to the score on the WISC-R (Wechsler Intelligence Scale for Children-Revised). He showed strong performance ability, but the verbal ability was down some. My husband and I were told that he was a Language Learning Disabled student. We were also told that he was probably dyslexic. He was placed in the resource room for one hour each day. This helped some, especially his attitude. When his attitude improved, he began to make some progress with reading, even though it was slow.

Sometime later, I was talking to a friend about my child. She had several children that had allergies. She started to tell me about the many reactions that her children had, and what could be done to help. Then she gave me the name of the doctor who gave her children allergy tests. She said that he used the "provocative food tests." This type of testing actually brings on the same reaction that would occur if the person ate the food.

At first, I thought that did not apply to Randy, but then I began to remember all of the strange things that had happened in his lifetime. I told my husband about this doctor and we decided to see if this could be the answer. We called for an appointment with the doctor. We were told that we would have to come for at least two days, if not more, for the first visit. Since this place is more than 100 miles from our home, we decided to go for three days. We had to stay in a motel. We would check in the doctor's office at 8 o'clock and stay until about 6 o'clock at night. We would have about an hour off to go to lunch.

The first day was very hard on Randy. At one point he fainted. There were many times the tests hurt, but he was very brave and tried not to show it. That evening, before we left the office, the nurse told him that she was going to give him a shot. She did and that was the first night that he slept without making so much noise with his nose and throat. Also, it was the first night, since birth, that he did not wet his bed. Randy was elated over this part. Also, he felt better since he had slept so well. He really looked forward to the next day and to taking more tests.

On the second day, the tests were all for food allergies. These went somewhat slower, but we found some very interesting reactions to some of the foods that Randy ate on a regular basis. That afternoon, the doctor examined Randy very carefully and then he told us that Randy did not have a real learning disability, but his brain was swelling due to some of the allergy reactions. He felt that when we got the allergies under control, Randy would not have this problem. We all realized that he would still be behind his peers, since he was starting 7th grade. At the same time we felt that with help he could make up some of this time and catch up with most of the things that his class was doing.

It was a struggle, but by the end of the 8th grade year, Randy was taken out of the special education class. He had made enough progress to work full time in the regular classroom. He advanced three years in his reading level in the 2 years of junior high school. This past year was his freshman year in high school. It has been exciting. He has a regular schedule and he played football. He had some trouble with a few subjects but he works on them. He does not have the desire to read like children who have learned to read at earlier ages. He can, however, read for information and/or comprehension. Many times his comprehension level is higher than other students, because he still reads slow, but he reads every word. Sometimes the faster reader is apt to skip something that is very important. It has helped his self-image to have the correct answers, when others are going back to look for them.

NOTE: Doylene Hogg is a graduate student in the Department of Special Education, Texas Woman's University at Denton.

NUTRITIONAL AND FEEDING PROBLEMS OF
THE PHYSICALLY HANDICAPPED

by Janine DiVincenti

An individual with a physical handicap may have difficulty consuming a nutritionally adequate diet because he/she is unable to feed himself/herself or he/she may be unable to chew food or swallow fluids and/or food. Examples of individuals who have special feeding problems are: an elderly person with arthritis; a person who has had a stroke; or a person with cerebral palsy. It is extremely important for the handicapped individual to beassisted in progressing to the highest possible level of independence in eating. When determining the method of feeding and/or the training to be used, it is necessary to assess the handicapped individual's needs for specific nutrients (protein, carbohydrate, fat, vitamins, and minerals). The individual's physical capacity must also be considered, and the following data examined: age, height, weight, sex, level of activity, and any special condition requiring dietary modification. It is important to become familiar with the individual's capacities in order to set realistic goals in a self-feeding training program.

Nutritional Needs

When a menu is planned for physically handicapped individual the Basic Four Food Groups is the starting point. If the person has a specific disease, the Basic Four Food Groups may not be appropriate to use. The diet may be altered for the individual according to his/her caloric needs. The consistency of the food must be appropriate for the individual's oral skills (chewing, swallowing, biting).

The Basic Four Food Groups consists of the Milk Group, the Meat Group, the Fruit-Vegetable Group and the Grain Group. The important nutrients supplied by foods in the Milk Group are found not only in milk to drink, but also in many varieties of cheese, cottage cheese, yogurt, ice cream, cream soups and puddings. These foods supply significant quantities of protein and calcium. Leafy green vegetables such as turnip greens, mustard greens, collard greens, and Kale are also good sources of calcium. The recommended number of servings to be consumed daily from this group is as follows: Adult - 2 servings; Child - 3 servings; Teenager - 4 servings; Pregnant Woman - 4 servings; Lactating Woman - 4 servings.

Meat, poultry, fish, and eggs contribute high quality protein, B vitamins, and iron to the diet. Significant sources of these nutrients are dry peas and beans (especially soybeans), and nurs. The recommended number of servings to be consumed each day is two servings for all individuals except pregnant women who need three servings.

The Fruit-Vegetable Group is important for its contribution of vitamin C and vitamin A to the diet. Four servings from the Fruit-Vegetable Group are recommended daily.

The Grain Group includes breads of all kinds, cereals, pastas, such as noodles, grits, and tortillas. This group supplied important amounts of B vitamins, iron and energy. Whole grain breads and cereals, especially those containing bran, also supply fiber which aids in regular elimination. It is recommended that four servings of foods from this group be consumed daily.

Other foods not included in the food groups are foods such as butter, margarine, vegetable oil, sugar, desserts such as cake, and condiments. The amounts of these foods included in the diet should be determined by the caloric needs of the handicapped individual. However, these foods should replace foods from the Four Food Groups.

Consistency Modification

The consistency of food is very important in assisting the handicapped individual who has difficulty with chewing and/or swallowing. Some handicapped individuals who have chewing or swallowing problems may need foods that are pureed. Those who have some chewing ability but who cannot eat solid food, such as a piece of roast beef, may require a diet with foods that are ground. Choking can be a problem if the consistency of the food is not appropriate for the individual.

Weight

Weight control is a very important consideration. Handicapped individuals whose activity is limited because of paralysis or another condition require a diet with adequate nutrients but without an excess of calories. Weight loss should be a goal for the obese handicapped individual, not only ti decrease the health risks associated with obesity but also to decrease the problems that caregivers may face in lifting the individual (as from a wheelchair to bed).

Underweight may also be a problem. The handicapped person with an athetoid condition (involuntary and irregular movements of the upper extremities) may need extra calories to make up for the excessive expenditure of energy.

Fluid

In addition to providing an adequate nutrient intake, providing an adequate fluid intake may also present a problem (1). There are those handicapped individuals who can take only small sips of fluid at one time. Those persons should be offered fluids at frequent intervals. If the individual is also receiving intravenous fluids, care must be taken so that he/she may not become over-dehydrated.

Constipation

If a handicapped individual must be given a blended diet because of chewing and/or swallowing problems, the diet most likely is also low in fiber (roughage). This factor, along with limited activity due to paralysis, may promote constipation. A plain brand cereal without raisins that has been allowed to soak in milk and then pureed in a blender can be given to those persons who can only take semi-liquid or blended foods. For those individuals who are sensitive to the slightest lumpy texture, this mixture may also need to be strained. Prune juice as well as cooked prunes without pits that have been blended and strained can also be used.

Menu Planning

The basic principles of meal planning should be kept in mind when planning menus for the physically handicapped individual. Variation in color, flavor, temperature, and texture (if possible) should be considered. It is not recommended to mix blended foods together unless the handicapped individual has verbalized a desire to have his/her foods combined.

The trend today is to allow the handicapped individual the opportunity to be as independent as possible and to do as much for himself/herself. It is the responsibility of the caregiver to provide such opportunities to promote this independence.

NOTE: Janine DiVincenti, R.D., is a Clinical Nutrition Specialist in the Food and Nutrition Services Department at Westgate Hospital and Medical Center, Denton, Texas.

REFERENCES

1. Mitchell, H.S., Hendrika J. Rynbergen, Linnea Anderson, & Marjorie Dibble. Nutrition in Health and Disease. 16th ed. Philadelphia: J.B. Lippincott Co., 1976.

2. _____. Nutrition Source Book. Rosemont, Illinois: National Dairy Council, 1978.

3. Manning, A.M. and Jeanne G. Means. A self-feeding program for geriatric patients in a skilled nursing home. Journal of the American Diabetic Association. 66:275, March 1975.

NUTRITION AND THE HANDICAPPED: NORMAL AND ABNORMAL
PROCESSES OF EATING

by Jean L. Judy

For a child to attain acceptable nutritional status, the mechanics for taking the nutrients must be adequate. In life threatening situations, artificial methods utilizing nasogastric Intravenous feeding, and gastronomy (direct tube feeding into the stomach) may be utilized. Long term usage of these methods creates many secondary problems, however, as well as depriving the individual of the satisfactions and stimulation derived from the process of eating. It is important, therefore, that caregivers exercise understanding, diligence, and patience in developing the most normal eating skills commensurate with the physiological needs and development of the child (4).

The purpose of this paper will be to aid the caregiver in his/her understanding of the reflexes associated with eating which are present in normal infants; to identify some possible abnormalities occurring when development is delayed; and to identify methods which may provide for remediation or adaption to the problems of the child with a developmental delay.

Reflexes and Developmental Sequence of Oral Functions

The normal neonate displays a high degree of efficiency in ingesting food from the breast or bottle. Aiding the baby in this accomplishment are several reflexive responses present at or shortly after birth (1). They are:

<u>Rooting</u>. (Birth to 3 months) Rooting is the turning of the head and opening of the mouth when the infant's cheek or lips are touched.

<u>Sucking</u>. (Appears at 4 or 5 months, remains throughout life). In mature sucking, the infant creates a vacuum in his mouth, sucking to bring fluids into his mouth through a nipple or straw.

<u>Chewing</u>. (Begins at 6 months) First in up and down motion, chewing develops a rotary component by 9 months, which permits the grinding of food as molars erupt.

<u>Tongue retraction</u>. (Appears at about 9 months) Tongue retraction allows the tongue to move to the back of the mouth, manipulating food and preparing it for swallowing. The tongue subsequently develops movements forward, to the side and up and down, which allows food to be retrieved from pockets in the mouth and cheeks, pushed between the teeth and positioned for swallowing. Once developed, these movements continue throughout life.

The progression of oral function is expected to occur in the normal infant as he/she is introduced to the graded textures of infant and adult foods, plus his own spontaneous exploration of the objects in his world many of which are brought to his mouth.

Problems of Developmental Delay and Techniques of Remediation

Children whose overall development is delayed due to central nervous system damage may exhibit delays in the development of oral functions. The result of this may be: (1) reflexes may persist for an abnormally long period of time or (2) establishing voluntary control may require special intervention and persistence for a long period of time.

Caregivers can stimulate normal eating patterns by applying techniques developed by occupational therapists which inhibit abnormal reflexes and facilitate lip closure, mature sucking, tongue movements and chewing.

The rooting reflex provides that the infant's head and mouth are brought into position for sucking. An acute sense of smell aids this orientation.

Suckling. (Birth to 3 months) This is an immature sucking reflex in which the lips are not closed in a tight seal. It can be elicited a few hours after birth by touching the lips or introducing a few drops of liquid into the baby's mouth.

Tongue protrusion. (Birth to 5 months) This pushing out of the tongue when food or an object is encountered in the mouth is a protective reflex. It can be observed when the mother introduces semi-solid food in the baby's diet and may be incorrectly interpreted by her as rejection of the food.

Suck-swallow. (Birth to 5 months) This pattern of sucking and immediately swallowing reflexively can be observed to continue even after the nipple of the baby's bottle collapses, and the milk flow is interrupted.

Bite reflex. (Birth to 5 or 7 months) This is an immediate, involuntary biting on anything this is introduced into the mouth.

Gag reflex. (Birth through life) The normal gagging reaction occurs when a stimulus is applied to the back of the tongue. The degree of sensitivity and area most responsive may vary from individual to individual, and may decrease with development.

As the nervous system of the infant develops, the reflexive responses are gradually replaced under voluntary control (1). The timing and sequence for this development occurs as follows:

Lip closure. (Appears at 4 or 5 months, remains throughout life) Lip closure brings the lips together firmly enough to form a seal, which allows the infant to remove food from a spoon, drink from a bottle or cup and prevents drooling.

Based on the knowledge of normal development sequences of eating, the caregiver should make an attempt to identify the problem areas, and should provide remediation only after careful observation.

Provide the necessary support. Positioning of the child should provide that the head is easily balanced over the trunk with the face forward and the neck slightly flexed. This allows the muscles of the face, jaw, lips, and throat to do their work of processing the food. Maintaining this alignment will be accomplished more easily if the hips, knees and ankles are flexed to approximately 90 degrees and given adequate support.

<u>Present the food</u>. Select a utensil appropriate for the size of the child's mouth, with a bowl that is shallow. Plastic coated spoons may be tolerated better than metal, if the child tends to bite on the spoons, or to have sensitive gums.

Touching the lips or letting the child smell the food will usually result in the mouth opening. Introduce small amounts of food into the midline of the mouth, press down slightly on the tongue behind the tip and wait for the lips to close. Food should never be scraped off onto the upper teeth. If lip closure does not occur after a few seconds, use the thumb and the index finger to close the lips, clearing the spoon.

For the child who is beginning to move the tongue from side to side, vary the placement of the food to either side. Present food that can be easily bitten (cooked carrots, small strips of vienna sausage) by placing the food between the molars, to encourage chewing.

Sucking which is absent or weak can be encouraged by several techniques.

<u>Straw drinking</u>. Offer liquids in a cup or glass with a short straw. If necessary, lightly press the child's lips around the straw, and manually stimulate sucking with a circular motion to the child's cheek. It may stimulate lip closure and sucking to adapt the straw by adding a plastic disc to contact the lips.

<u>Lip closure</u>. Lip closure may be strengthened during meal times in the following manner: When the child has completed the sequence for removing food from the spoon, chewing and swallowing, removal of food from the lips and chin should be done by brisk blotting and pressing of the lips in a direction away from the mouth. This stretching of the muscle around the mouth will encourage a pursing response, building the muscle used in lip closure.

<u>Choosing the foods</u>. Food is a strong stimulus. The child responds not only to the smell of food (by lifting his/her head, opening his/her mouth and turning toward the stimulus) he/she also responds to the flavor and texture. Foods of a progressively firm texture should be presented to the child who is developing oral functions. Beginning with semi-solids of the texture of mashed potatoes, apple sauce, or pureed foods of gradually more demanding texture should be introduced. A wide variety of firm, chewable foods should be used to assure nutritional adequacy and to accustom the child to a wide variety of temperatures, textures and flavors. Introduce only the one new food at a time, in small amounts, when the child is hungry. Observe closely, taking advantage of his readiness to progress. The food that requires biting should be placed between the molars with just enough in the mouth so that the bite-sized piece may be moved about and chewed before being swallowed.

Physical Problems of Self-Feeding and Utensil Adaptations

Before attempting to teach the child self-feeding, it is necessary to assess his/her readiness for this activity. In addition to acquiring the oral functions of lip closure, sucking, swallowing and biting and chewing, the child should demonstrate the ability to maintain his head in alignment with his trunk while sitting, and bring his hand to his mouth with some ability to grasp a utensil or to pick up small bits of food.

The success of a self feeding program depends upon many factors, including the child's understanding, motivation, and physical ability. Adapted utensils may be useful in the event that a lack of physical ability is the principal limiting factor. There are many adapted devices on the market; others can be devised to meet specific needs. Problems for which adapted utensils may be most useful include poor grasp, poor upper extremity strength, and poor co-ordination of hand to mouth movements.

Problems of poor grasp may be solved by utensils with built up handles, held in grasp with the fingers and thumb around the handle. A loop handle passing around the child's palm, into which the handle of a fork or spoon is inserted may also be used. Cups with handles on both sides or small lightweight cups are easily grasped by the child who needs to use both hands. A single handle on the cup may be a sufficient aid for the child with poor grasp.

When upper extremity strength is limited or trunk balance is poor, raising the height of the table may aid the child in his/her self feeding efforts.

Poor co-ordination may require that the plate or bowl be stabilized by placing it on a piece of damp foam or on a rubber or plastic mat. Plates with suction cups attached to the underside are available commercially, and may provide the needed stability. A scoop guard plater further aids the child with poor co-ordination.

This paper has discussed the normal developmental sequence of oral functions, some abnormal conditions that may be encountered in children with developmental delay and some methods of overcoming or adapting to the feeding problems of handicapped children.

Examination of problems of eating and determining solutions appropriate to a specific individual may require the skills of an occupational therapist, speech pathologist, nurse or nutritionist specializing in this area. Caregivers are called upon to understand the normal sequence, identify problem areas by careful observation, provide the most normal eating experience of which the child is capable, record results carefully and persist with patience and understanding as the individual matures in oral function and in efforts of self feeding.

NOTE: Jean L. Judy, MA, OTR, is an Instructor in the School of Occupational Therapy at Texas Woman's University at Denton.

REFERENCES

1. Coley, I.L. <u>Pediatric Assessment of Self Care Activities</u>.
   C.V. Mosby Co., 1978.

2. Fiorentino, M. <u>Normal and Abnormal Development</u>. 2nd Ed.
   Charles Thomas Co., 1976.

3. Gaffney, T.W., & Campbell, R. Feeding Techniques for Dysphagic
   Patients, <u>American Journal of Nursing</u>, 74:12, Dec., 1972.

4. Mitchell, H.S., et. al. <u>Nutrition in Health and Disease</u>.
   Sixth Edition, Chapter 24, J.B. Lippincott Co., 1976.

5. Pearson, P. & Williams, C. (eds.) <u>Physical Therapy Services in the Developmental Disabilities</u>. Chapter 6 by Helen Mueller, Charles C. Thomas Co., 1972.

PARENT COUNSELING:
PROFESSIONAL VIEW AND PARENTAL REACTION

by Donna L. Sumlin and Jamy Black McCole

Only a few years ago the terms "parent counseling" and/or "parent training" were known and used by only a handful of professionals who recognized the need for parents experiencing "normal" problems encountered in child-rearing as being deserving of therapeutic intervention. For countless generations it was generally believed that one possessed "parenting skills" adequate to assume the role of parent at the precise moment of the child's birth and as the two proud individuals were officially proclaimed "mother" and "daddy." Contrary to this popular and somewhat mythological belief, has emerged the notion that few rites of passage bear the consequence and carry with them the far reaching impact as does the decision to raise children. However, society as a whole has failed to create the necessary institutions to help individuals adjust to and cope with their dramatically altered lifestyle that accompanies the decision to become a parent. Likewise, society has also failed to provide any type of tangible incentive or encouragement in the form of emotional support to couples anticipating parenthood. For the most part, parenthood as portrayed through the mass media of television, newspapers, and magazines is a world of fantasy where the emphasis is on a state of continual bliss and happiness. Parents are erroneously depicted as fountains of wisdom, understanding, love, intellect, wit, charm as well as vocationally successful and financially secure. Children on the other hand, are generally characterized as physically attractive, charmingly precocious, intellectually gifted, loving, and mature enough to be trusted with responsibility at an early age. Unfortunately, for many prospective parents this distorted fantasy based portrayal of parenthood is the primary model of behavior available to them. It is not until after the child's birth that the discrepancy between what is portrayed by the mass media as "normal" and "ideal" and the actual "realities" of parenting begin to produce emotional conflict for the new parents. It is at this juncture that many parents experience guilt and anxiety because they do not resemble the model presented them.

If, as the previous passage suggests, that parenting is learned from such sources as the mass media, and certainly one's own parent models, and if what is learned is a somewhat distorted picture of what a parent is "suppose to be," then what is being offered on the subject of parenting to parents of disabled children? Unfortunately, at this point in time, relatively little or in many instances nothing! The parent of the disabled child is being required to generalize that which is learned about parenting a child without a disability to the child with a disability. Some may respond by saying, "But what is wrong with that?" The answer is both simple and complex. First, the needs of the disabled child are unique and call for unique and often complicated solutions. Secondly, the parent of the disabled child must deal with a diverse and often differing set of attitudes toward the "self," intra-personal attitudes and attitudes toward the "child," or inter-personal attitudes. And, finally, the methods and strategies employed by the parent of the child without a disability to foster ongoing healthy development are not always effective with the disabled child, e.g., discipline, acquisition of motor skills, development of social-emotional maturity, independence, responsibility, etc.

It seems logical to assume that if parents are to truely be effective and competent in their role of parent then we must also assume that some type of preparation and/or training for parenthood is needed. This would certainly seem to apply to the parent of the disabled child. In reality, the assumption that training and/or counseling is needed by the majority of parents with a disabled child in order to assist them in successfully fulfilling their unique role as well as meeting the unusual demands often placed upon them is quite accurate. Of course, it has to be admitted, that it is virtually impossible to train all new parents to be prepared for the prospect of being the parent of a disabled child nor is it desirable to provide such training prior to the birth of a child when it is not known whether or not the child will be disabled. However, it is possible, feasible, and definately desirable to counsel with parents of disabled children in order to enhance and facilitate their functioning as effective, knowledgeable, and emotionally well adjusted caregivers.

Many of you may be saying to yourself, "I'm a teacher or PT/OT therapist, I won't be counseling parents as a routine part of my job." Nothing could be further from the truth. Any time that you work with a disabled child you will also be working with and counseling that child's parents. Perhaps it might be useful to provide a working definition of counseling. Very simply defined, counseling may be referred to as a helping process in which one individual attempts to help another. It involves dynamic interaction between two individuals with the goal being to enhance self-worth, contribute to personal growth, and/or to remediate problem areas. It should be readily apparent that a counseling relationship can and often is established in all types of situation and under varied circumstances. The preceeding definition suggests that at some time in our lives we will all be called upon to assume the role of counselor. It also becomes obvious, that those of us working with disabled children and their parents, in whatever capacity, will find themselves frequently thrust into the role of counselor.

Although it is not the purpose of this presentation to examine various counseling techniques, it might be useful to remember the following points when working with parents of disabled children.

Counseling, especially parent counseling, involves the exploration and sharing of feelings with the goal being to increase awareness of intra- and inter-personal functioning which can be evidenced by positive changes in attitudes toward the "self" and the "disabled child" in the family. Likewise, in any helping relationship the therapy functions of permissiveness, orientation to reality, catharsis, mutual trust, caring, understanding, acceptance, and support are involved.

At this time counseling parents of disabled children is receiving increased attention as the result of such Federal legislation as Public Law 94-142 (14) and the relatively new piece of legislation Public Law 95-602. The latter amends the 1973 Rehabilitation Act and states among other things, that model research and demonstration programs must be established for the provision of appropriate services for parents of disabled children - including parent counseling and training. (15) When viewed in perspective, the history of parent counseling is relatively brief when compared to other groups receiving specialized treatment. It was not until the late 1930s and early 1940s that such noted professionals as Adler, Slavson, Amster, and Kolodney (4, 12, 1, 7) began to recognize the crucial role of the parent in the treatment of emotionally disturbed children. Finally, psychotherapists were beginning to acknowledge the need to include the parent in treatment as well as the child and to recognize an inter-relationship between the child's behavior and parental attitudes and behavior. Despite the fact that psychotherapists were beginning to see a need for counseling parents of emotionally disturbed children, it has not manifested itself until only recently when these and other professionals have begun to counsel parents of children with varying disabling conditions.

While the majority of the presentation will be devoted to an examination of parents' views on the benefits to be derived from parent counseling, a brief portion will involve the exploration of emotional reactions frequently experienced by parents of disabled children. Traditionally, the primary goal of parent counseling has been to help parents adjust to and cope with their unique role. Developing insight and understanding by the parent of the numerous reactions such as shock, grief, bewilderment, disbelief, guilt as well as many others has been an integral part of the counseling process. To a great extent, the emphasis of counseling has been on the psychodynamics underlying the various emotional reactions experienced by these parents. In recent years this emphasis has begun to shift and has been replaced by a substantially broadened concept of parent counseling. Today parent counseling does not deal soley with the intra-psychic conflicts exhibited by these parents, it now involves training of parents in methods of child guidance appropriate for use with their disabled child as well as acquainting them with information regarding community resources serving their needs. Although each of these areas of parent counseling deserve special attention, this presentation will focus only on the intrapsychic conflicts experience by this population of parents as well as their attitudes toward counseling.

Most authorities in the area of counseling would agree that initial parental attitudes and concomitant behavioral reactions have a profound impact on the parent-child relationship, especially between a parent and a disabled child. It is not an exaggeration to state that parents of disabled children have been presented with one of life's greatest challenges and that everything they are or hope to be will find expression in their relationship with that child and influence the manner in which the child is raised.

It is readily apparent that parental attitudes toward their disabled children are significantly influenced by their attitudes and perceptions of themselves. In other words, parents' perceptions of their own worth as well as their evaluations of other persons and events are influenced by the variations in the physical, intellectual and psychological characteristics of their children. Thus, parents intra-personal, or attitudes toward the "self" are not only engendered by the child's disability, they are a direct reaction to the disability.

A primary emotional reaction found to be experienced by nearly all parents of disabled children is guilt. Although guilt has many causes and whether it is real or imagined, it is quite often related to feelings that poor or inadequate care was provided either during the prenatal period or during infancy (16). Guilt has also been found to result from feelings of anger and hostility directed toward the child as well as from impulses to reject the child. Not infrequently, guilt has been exhibited by parents who have an unwanted child who turns out to be disabled.

Combined with feelings of guilt are attitudes of self-blame or feelings of being at fault for having caused the child's disabling condition. Likewise, feelings of shame for having produced such a child may develop and be manifested in overt self-consciousness. This devalued parental role is often associated with the social stigma attached to the child's disability which in turn is communicated to the child (10). This social stigma is often related to society's emphasis on intelligence and is at times compounded by irrational fears of a "tainted" family history which together contribute to feelings of personal worthlessness (9, 11). It has also been found that the parents' attempt to fulfill societal expectations has a tremendous impact on their self-esteem. Low self-esteem is not uncommon among these parents as a disabled child is a blow to the pride of accomplishment. One comment that was repeated often by parents suggested that in order for a counseling relationship to be effective...

Counselors need empathy

On the subject of group counseling parents seemed to have mixed emotions, especially with regard to the counselor's role:

> It can really hurt when a counselor isn't objective or doesn't lead the group.

The following statements clearly indicate the parents' need to be with other parents who share similar problems:
* Children are all so individual, but it is helpful to talk to another parent with a disabled child.
* It is good to have other parents of disabled children to talk to for support and as a sounding board.
* You can say things to parents of disabled children that other parents would not understand.
* It helps to alleviate some of the feelings about being sick of your kid - which would mortify some others to hear a parent of a disabled child say - about that poor little kid.
* Society in general doesn't understand the feelings of parents of disabled children.
* It can be so helpful to be around parents of older disabled children than your own.

Parents were very vocal and did not hesitate to express strong feelings about the difficulty involved in obtaining various needed services:
* I found that I needed to be informed myself in order to ask for appropriate services but then they were ready to help on what I requested after they checked out what I had told them.
* I find I must be very informed to tell the professional what my child should receive - this should be the professional's responsibility but I find I must know.
* Everyone's uncoordinated in their services - in their own world.
* We have to fight for the kids or they will be hidden like they use to be.
* I use to be passive but found out that I had to decide to speak up and let them get mad if needed.
* It's an emotional drain to call places and search for all these services.

In this context the child is regarded as an externalization, a demonstration to the world the parents' self-concept of basic inferiority. A common defense against this feeling of inferiority is a search for an explanation for the situation, an explanation which will not only preserve self-esteem, but will also absolve the parent of feelings of guilt.

Another kind of guilt that is not uncommon among these parents is the kind that stems from the belief that the disabled child was sent as either a punishment from God for some past transgression, or an act of God, entrusting the parents to provide the best possible care (8). Guilt has been found frequently to be a contributing factor to marital problems as partners blame each other for their problems or feel personally "defective" or responsible for their situation (13).

While the preceeding portion of this presentation has been

devoted to an examination of some of the emotional reactions experienced by parents of disabled children, it has also been an examination of those reactions most frequently encountered by the professional as s/he assists the parent in therapy. In order to obtain a different perspective on parent counseling, the remainder of this presentation will be an exploration of the parents' attitudes toward counseling and caregiving of the disabled child. The following statements were obtained during numerous counseling sessions with parents whose children possessed a variety of disabling conditions as well as represented a wide age range.

With respect to the parents past experiences in counseling, the following remarks were made:

*I think counselors need to really care instead of merely demanding certain answers and feelings from parents.

*When counselors are experienced in working with parents they are better than those with just book-learning.

*The good side to it is that it builds confidence when you do know how to get around - it raises your consciousness.

Parental ambivalence regarding future expectations of their disabled children is openly expressed by such comments as:

*We've been told by so many professionals that he won't do this and he can't do that, that I think at times why try? But I have to set some goals and he has mastered sitting up.

*I don't want to rely on professionals opinions but I find that I do - I am afraid to expect things but afraid not to.

*With others that deal with my child, like at school, I try to get them to push as hard as I am - I check around and get my child put in a class where I know he'll be challenged.

The opinions and feelings expressed by the preceeding parent comments reflect only a small portion of the varied emotional and physical stress placed on their shoulders as the result of being the parent of a disabled child. For these parents, each new day, each new developmental milestone brings with it a new set of challenges and a new set of problems to deal with constructively. The delights and achievements of childhood are often measured in minute steps which to an outsider might not even be visable. However, these parents of disabled children, if given proper guidance and provided adequate services can become contributing partners with professionals serving the disabled child in the family.

NOTE: Donna Sumlin is an Education Specialist with the U.S. Department of Navy, Corpus Christi, Texas. Jamy McCole is Executive Director of the United Cerebral Palsy Association in Ft. Worth, Texas.

REFERENCES

1. Amster, F., "Collective Psychotherapy of Mothers of Emotionally Disturbed Children," *American Journal of Orthopsychiatry*, 14 (January, 1944), 44-52.

2. Bruch, Hilde, "The Role of the Parent in Psychotherapy with Children," *Psychiatry*, 11 (1948), 169-175.

3. Cummings, S. Thomas, Helen G. Bayley, and Herbert E. Rie, "Effects of the Child's Deficiency on the Mothers of Mentally Retarded, Chronically Ill and Neurotic Children," *American Journal of Orthopsychiatry*, 36 (July, 1966), 595-608.

4. Deutsch, Danica, "A Multiple Approach to Child Guidance," *Journal of Individual Psychology*, 13 (May - November), 171-175.

5. Gilberg, Arnold L., "The Stress of Parenting," *Child Psychology and Human Development*, 6 (Winter, 1975), 59-67.

6. Heisler, Verda, "Dynamic Group Psychotherapy with Parents of Cerebral Palsied Children," *Rehabilitation Literature*, 35 (November, 1974), 329-330.

7. Kolodney, E., "Treatment of Mothers in a Group as a Supplement to Child Psychotherapy," *Mental Hygiene*, 28 (July, 1944), 437-444.

8. Love, Harold D., *Parental Attitudes Toward Exceptional Children*, Springfield, Illinois, Charles C. Thomas, 1970.

9. Michaels, J. and H. Schucman, "Observations on the Psychodynamics of Parents of Retarded Children," *American Journal of Mental Deficiency*, 66 (January, 1962), 568-573.

10. Milman, Doris H., "Group Therapy with Parents: An Approach to the Rehabilitation of Physically Disabled Children," *Journal of Pediatrics*, 41 (July, 1952), 113-116.

11. Schucman, Helen, "Further Observations on the Psychodynamics of Parents of Retarded Children," *Training School Bulletin*, 60 (August, 1963), 70-74.

12. Slavson, S.R., *Child-Centered Group Guidance of Parents*, New York, International Universities Press, 1974.

13. Stone, Marguerite M., "Parental Attitudes to Retardation," *American Journal of Mental Deficiency*, 53 (October, 1948), 363-372.

14. U.S. Congress, Public Law 94-142, Washington, Government Printing Office, 1975.

15. U.S. Congress, Public Law 95-602, Washington, Government Printing Office, 1978.

16. Wolfensberger, W., Counseling the Parents of the Retarded," Edited by A.A. Baumeister, Mental Retardation: Appraisal, Education, and Rehabilitation, Chicago, Illinois, Aldine, 1967.

UNION C.C.
CRANFORD, NJ 07016